D1250925

THE LAND SYSTEM
OF THE UNITED STATES

The Land System of the United States

An Introduction to the History and Practice
of Land Use and Land Tenure

By

MARION CLAWSON

UNIVERSITY OF NEBRASKA PRESS · LINCOLN

Publishers on the Plains

UNP

Copyright © 1968 by the University of Nebraska Press

All Rights Reserved

Library of Congress Catalog Card Number: 68–10250

Manufactured in the United States of America

Foreword

This volume is based on Marion Clawson, *Man and Land in the United States* (Lincoln: University of Nebraska Press, 1964), which was redrafted to serve as an introduction to the United States land system for foreign readers.

The publication was initiated and sponsored by the North Central Land Economics Research Committee, a group representing the Departments of Agricultural Economics at the State Universities of Alaska, Illinois, Indiana, Iowa, Kansas, Kentucky, Michigan, Minnesota, Missouri, Nebraska, North Dakota, Ohio, South Dakota, and Wisconsin; the Farm Foundation of Chicago; and the Economic Research Service of the United States Department of Agriculture.

Work on the publication was carried out mainly through the subcommittee on World Land Tenure. Folke Dovring served as chairman of the subcommittee.

Contents

List of Illustrations

ILLUSTRATION CREDITS

Acknowledgment is given to the following sources that have provided illustrative material used in this book: Drawn especially for this book by Federal Graphics—Figures 1, 2, 7, 10, and 22. Provided by the Bureau of Land Management, Department of the Interior—Figures 3 and 4. Used by permission of Dodd, Mead & Co. from *Uncle Sam's Acres* (1951)—Figures 5, 6, 8, and 9. Used by permission of The Johns Hopkins Press from *The Federal Lands: Their Use and Management* (1957) —Figure 21; and from *Land for the Future* (1960)—Figure 18. Used by permission of Rand McNally & Co. from *Land for Americans* (1963)— Figures 12, 14, 16, 18, and 19. Figure 11 is from *United States Census of Agriculture, 1959,* "A Graphic Summary of Land Utilization," Vol. 5, Pt. 6, chapt. 1, p. 17. Figure 15 is from *United States Census of Agriculture, 1954,* "A Graphic Summary of Farm Tenure, 1954," Vol. 3, Pt. 4, chapt. 3, p. 141.

CHAPTER 1

Land System and Social System

Throughout the long ages of history and prehistory, people have depended upon land for all their material needs. How large resources a country has in its land depends in part upon the technology applied. As civilization rose, soil and subsoil, rocks and water, air and sunshine became greater and greater resources, in response to more and more productive technology. Yet, before the Industrial Revolution, the resources in the Old World allowed no more than a bare minimum subsistence for most people, for population tended to increase as fast as the resource base. The well-known Malthusian circle of events produced an ever sharper competition for the use and control of land and other natural resources. The sharper the competition, the more crucial was the legal and social system of control. In a land-based society, the land system was decisive for the whole kind of society, economy, and culture that could exist.

In modern time this has been modified. A mature urban-industrial society produces most of its national income through processing of raw materials; the raw materials themselves are but a tiny fraction of the national product. This makes many people believe that land is less important than it once was. In a sense this is true, for the new, high-productive industrial and agricultural technologies have made us less restricted in our choices by the natural environment. The competition for direct control of land is also not always as fierce as it used to be. But in another and deeper sense we are as dependent upon the land as ever, for its products are basic to our whole way of life. If people in general do not feel that the land system is a problem to them,

1

then this just means that the system is well adapted to current needs. If it were inadequate to service society and its productive and consumptive purposes, then we would be more aware of how basic land is to our existence. The most critical angles of the land question in the United States today are in the large cities with their complex space and transportation problems, and in the increasing demand for outdoor living which many people have come to value more and more for the rest and recreation it gives. The farm land system, on the whole, works smoothly and better than in most other countries.

This land system is the main topic of this volume—how it came about, how it has worked in the past and how it works now, and what are its perspectives for the future. Emphasis is on farm land. The related subjects of forest lands, urban land, and public lands are treated as adjuncts to the central topic of the farm land system. Technology is treated inasmuch as it affects the land system, but the central theme is the land system itself: titles and records, ownership distribution, tenure, patterns of use, etc. The history and characteristics of the land system in the United States are described here with a view to allow comparisons with other land systems in the world. The purpose is not to recommend copying the United States institutions in any other country, regardless of local conditions. Our purpose is, rather, to show by the example of the United States land system how crucially important the choice of land institutions is, especially for the formative phase of transition from a rural to an urban-industrial economy and society.

The kind of land tenure system (laws and customs) that people create and use depends in part on their natural environment. In an arid climate, for instance, they are likely to have different laws relating to the use of water than they will have in a humid climate. But usually the systems of land tenure and land use are affected much more by a people's basic philosophy and culture than by the natural environment. The basic philosophy may find expression, for instance, in the rules about in-heritage and will (testament). What a person may decide about his property after his death varies from country to country, but in each country, the rules in force are usually taken for granted; they say something about the people's attitude and opinion in regard to the rights of individuals. Contrasts such as those between private property and Communistic property represent extremes only; within private property systems there are many shades as to just how far the individual is protected against society and vice versa.

The American value systems cannot be treated in detail here; they are referred to in passing when required. The following chapters show how the American philosophy, as far as it relates to land, evolved and changed from the earliest colonial times to the present. Much of this philosophy about land has remained relatively constant, but there have been some changes, and in particular there have been changes in the way certain philosophies were worked out in practice.

American land history is dramatic, at least to those who know it well. Small groups of colonists landed on a strange coast and managed to survive and increase in spite of great hardships and many setbacks. Coming from the Old World where nearly all land was occupied, they found before them an entirely new situation: land that was vacant for their purposes. The early colonists were to a great extent people who were dissatisfied with conditions in their old country and determined to build a new society which would make their pent-up ambitions evolve into reality. Often there was divergence or even conflict within their ranks as to these aims and how to achieve them. The exploration and settlement of the continent is one of the most exciting chapters of world history—trappers, traders, frontiersmen, cattlemen, homesteaders, miners, and many others cross the pages of history as the big push of a new society rolled westward. Everywhere it was land which drew them on, which held them in hospitable spots, and which engaged their greatest energies and deepest interests.

3

The Revolution, the acquisition of the Louisiana Purchase, the other great territorial additions, the disposal of the new public lands to settlers—and to speculators—are all colorful parts of American history. The situation of the settler country differed from that of the Old World in this crucial respect: land was not scarce in any decisive sense. People were the scarce resource, despite the fact that the consequences of the Industrial Revolution did not arrive in quantity until much of the new society had already taken shape. Some of those consequences, moreover, arrived very much in time to permit the new expanses of the Midwest and Far West to be tied to the East by effective communication systems. With the old Malthusian law temporarily out of function, land settlement in North America became almost perfectly timed to a transition from agrarian to urban-industrial life without any intervening period of massive proletarian poverty. These fortunate circumstances have, of course, been powerful in promoting the growth and development of American society and economy which took place. But alone by themselves they are not sufficient to explain it. Comparison with other settler countries, in South America for instance, will show that a generous fund of vacant land does not produce the kind of economic and societal growth experienced in the United States, unless the expansion takes place through suitable institutional arrangements. The basis for America's greatness was in the combination of vast resources with institutions which, for all their human faults, were adequate to handle the situation.

Land history is also human history, and behind the account of the build-up and the changes in land institutions, the reader will have to imagine the human strength and foibles of those who carried these developments. To understand the United States of today, knowledge of its land history is essential. The rush to settle the "West"—from Ohio to California—produced some essential characteristics of the American people: its strong adherence to private property as well as the partly contrasting high rate of mobility, for instance; and these influences do not

4

fade out as quickly as the settlement and occupational patterns change.

More than two thirds of the people of the United States now live in cities and, as population increases, so does the share of the cities in the total. The relation of these people to the land of the farmer becomes more and more indirect. Their food is bought in highly processed form, and so are most other necessities or luxuries. Even the proportion of those who own their own home in the form of one-family dwellings is a declining portion of the total. In this advanced industrial civilization, few individuals can retain the degree of material self-sufficiency which characterized—or was thought to characterize—the farmer of a past age which is only two or three generations removed from ours. The farmers who grew most of their own food and whose diets were partly determined by what they grew; who kept sheep to produce their own wool, which they carded, spun, and wove into cloth from which clothing was made; who cured hides from the animals they slaughtered, to make the shoes they needed; who cut from their own woods the logs from which houses and furniture were made, and which provided the fuel to heat their houses—all of this was typical of a hundred and fifty years ago in the United States. Some of it, some people can remember who still belong to the active generations of today.

And yet, the independence of each other which these people enjoyed was more apparent than real, for it hinged on the existence of strong, individualistic institutions, which the community was prepared to uphold, as well as on defense and political arrangements which could only exist because of the measure of economic exchange and foreign trade that had developed. The difference against the deep-seated interdependence of today is therefore one of degree, and the same is true of the apparent lesser dependence on land. But if the individual who buys his groceries, his clothes, etc., in the stores has little direct concern with the tenure conditions on the farms that produce the raw

5

materials—and produce them in abundance enough to keep large surplus stocks to make famine unthinkable in peace time —then this is also a measure of how hard he might be hit if the quiet working of the land system were to be interrupted or disturbed. The land area a modern person uses directly and exclusively is small, but indirectly or jointly with others he uses vast areas of land—fractions of all the farms and mine sites from which his necessities and luxuries draw their raw material; the streets and roads on which he circulates; the public buildings and the private businesses which he uses or which service him; the recreation areas to which he goes frequently or seldom. All told, the land system of the whole country concerns the individual in some degree. In one way or the other, this will always be so.

CHAPTER 2

Early Colonization

The colonization of North America by settlers from Europe was not merely a result of the discovery of the new lands on the Western Hemisphere. The Spaniards left most of the northern continent untouched, and the first successful English settlement came more than a century after the great discovery. The attraction of vacant land needed the response of dynamic forces in Europe to have any consequence. When many Europeans left for America out of dissatisfaction with conditions at home, then this reflects the historical principle that revolutions are made to accelerate ongoing change rather than to start new trends. The early colonies in North America were founded by men and women who wanted to build new societies; they wanted to bring to fruition aspirations which were new also in the old continent, rocked with political and religious upheavals and rife with the ferment of new ideas. These kinds of aspirations were profoundly different from those of the Spanish *conquistadores*. The colonists also met a different geographic environment which presented more of a challenge to those who wanted to found a new society. By its scope and consequences, the early colonization of North America is unique in world history. The specific ways in which it took place explain much in the history that followed, including the central role that land institutions came to play.

Colonists came to the area now included in the United States from several countries of western Europe—France, Germany, Holland, Sweden, Spain, and others. In this chapter, however, we shall consider only the role of the colonists from Britain.

7

There are several reasons for this emphasis. British settlers comprised a large part of all the early colonists, and all of the colonies that eventually united to form the United States were ruled by England for a comparatively long period of time. British ideas on land use, land ownership, and land tenure came to dominate the colonial experience. Other colonists have also left traces upon land use and land tenure, as for instance the Dutch in New York State and the Spaniards in the Southwest. But these are minor features compared to the mainstream of British influence.

WHAT THE EARLY COLONISTS
LEFT BEHIND

The ferment of new ideas in Europe was well timed to the new opportunities overseas. This was no mere coincidence. The new art of sailing across the oceans was part of the early rise in arts and sciences as well as of the kind of economic enterprise typified by early capitalism. Reformation, the printing press, strong monarchial government, and the libertarian thinking of the Renaissance all did their part to wreck the societal forms of the Middle Ages. The feudal institutions of medieval Europe were in full decay when America was discovered and they had all but disappeared when North America was colonized, but in their wake most European areas still had sharp class distinctions and complicated land tenure systems. If the North American land system can be said to mark a clean break with the land systems associated with feudalism, then this was merely an acceleration of tendencies in the old countries, where the vestiges of feudalism were moribund. It is only logical that this revolt should come to fruition earliest in the new country, where there was less of the inertia which allows entrenched institutions to outlive their rationale.

Any strong trend of change has its countercurrents, and the rise of commercial wealth in the cities of Europe met with two

8

powerful ones. One was the reaction of the landed gentry to solidify their institutions into the closed ranks of inheritable nobility; the conflicts provoked by this were resolved only through the upheavals of the French Revolution. The other countercurrent, which came later, stemmed from the paradox that the new ideas, the new technology, and the new opportunity created by the great geographic discoveries, all contributed to an unprecedented increase in population—the first installment of the modern "population explosion." Before modern industrial technology was invented, let alone came to maturity, this demographic increase led to increased well-being only for a few on the top of the social ladder; for the masses it meant, if anything, more severe individual poverty. Such changes could only sharpen and prolong inherited class distinctions; at the time, only a few visionaries dreamt of the day when economic well-being would become general.

The living conditions of the seventeenth and eighteenth centuries bear, of course, no comparison with those of modern America or Europe, and such comparison is also not needed to explain what happened. The people of those days did not measure with the yardstick of a distant future; the happier parts of their contemporary world were enough to inspire effort and concerted action. The "revolution of rising expectations" of those days was keyed to the vacant land and the free horizon of newly discovered continents rather than to the higher productivity of new technology as is true in the underdeveloped countries today. Despite the strength of this attraction, few people actually migrated across the ocean in the seventeenth and eighteenth centuries. Sailing was not only much more insecure than in the age of the steamship; its total physical capacity was also small, and the cost per person high, witness the terms of contract for "indentured servants." The size of the population in the colonies, at the eve of independence, seems to have been due more to high birth rate and moderate death rate than to any large influx of people. In a sense this, too, reflects the incipient

9

character of the tendencies of a modern economy in Europe. To the rural masses America long remained a mirage. It became a reality most of all for the ocean-sailing nations, such as England and Holland. The Swedes in Delaware and the French in Quebec did not migrate; they were brought there. Much of the early colonization stemmed from religious trouble in Britain, where nonconformists fled the reactionary policies of James I and Charles I, and Catholic "cavaliers" fled from the dictatorship of Oliver Cromwell to settle in Maryland. By the peculiar logic in the theology of those days, religious freedom, in most cases, meant freedom for their own church. Most people did not hesitate to suppress others who differed with them, even as they had been suppressed at home. Others sought economic and political opportunity—again for themselves, certainly not for all mankind; such an idea would have been premature at that time. The attraction of land was strong, for despite the new economic features in Europe, all of its countries still had a land-based economy, and increased commerce would need increased production foremost of the things that land can produce. The revolt against aristocratic land institutions in the old country would not of itself preclude attempts at building new aristocratic institutions overseas, as typified by the southern tobacco and cotton estates. What salvaged the new settlements from repeating the mistakes and the oppression of the old continent were two things: the polycentricism which was a consequence of the immense spaces available for settlement, and the vastness of this space itself, which defied any attempt at a land monopoly or a close regimentation of people.

WHAT THE EARLY COLONISTS FOUND IN THE NEW COUNTRY

The new colonists to North America found a strange and primitive land, different from what they had known at home and difficult to adjust to.

10

The climate was rougher than in the old country. In contrast to western Europe with its predominantly maritime influence upon the weather, North America with its north-south mountain systems is open to the sharply contrasting influences of the tropical heat of the Caribbean Sea on the one hand and of the Canadian arctic on the other, causing abrupt short-range variations in temperature and humidity as well as sharp contrasts between the seasons.

Coming from fully settled open country dominated by ploughland and pasture as in England and Holland, the colonists found forests everywhere. With few exceptions, the eastern half of the United States was originally forested, even though many local clearings had resulted from the Indians' farming. The primeval forests were magnificent—huge trees, large, straight, and tall, with many more species than are naturally found in Europe. The forests seemed endless; explorers on horseback or on foot could go for days without seeing any substantial clearing. To the new settlers, these forests were both a blessing and a menace. They provided materials for buildings and furniture and many other articles, as well as fuel for heating. In a later phase, settlers in New England and Canada could supply the British warships and merchant vessels with vital supplies such as masts and tar.

In many ways the forest was a hindrance. It had to be cleared away before the land could be farmed. Removing a single specimen of these stately hardwood trees was a big job with the tools at hand, and the huge stumps could be removed only with the greatest difficulty. Many settlers "girdled" the trees, letting them die and decay naturally, while farming among the dead trees or their stumps. This technique the white settlers learned from Indians. Coherent arable tracts were created only after several years. Clearing a few acres was often the work of years. As trouble with Indians came up in one area after another, the forest was dreaded as the harboring place from which the Indians attacked the little settlements.

11

This early experience of forests led to popular attitudes where the forests were at best tolerated; many people continued to dislike or even hate them. Their value was taken for granted and their availability in the future was assumed to be indefinite. These attitudes, ingrained from early days, were to linger on after the situations that had called them into being had long ceased to exist.

The early settlers found no roads anywhere, nor were decent roads built for many decades. The Indians had some trails that could be used for foot and horseback travel. Most movement of people and goods had to be by water, either along the coast or on the small streams. The ocean-going ships of those days were very small by modern standards and could often penetrate up the larger rivers for considerable distances. They could go up the Chesapeake Bay and the Potomac River, for instance, and load tobacco right from the planter's small wharf. The lack of good transport facilities was serious, yet much less so in the age of near self-sufficiency than in a more commercialized society. Water was still the chief element of transportation also in Europe, and to this day it is the cheapest one for bulky goods.

Even before any towns could be founded, settlements were clustered in groups which were called "towns" in those days. People built their houses close together for protection and sociability, and thus the early settlements resembled small villages rather than the system of isolated farmsteads which came to dominate the westward expansion.

If North America seemed a vacant land to the settlers from Europe, yet all of it was occupied, after a fashion, by the Indians. Indian culture at the time varied greatly and was not entirely untouched by European culture; the horse, which is often thought of as characteristic of Indian way of life, had been brought to the continent by the Spaniards. Some Indians practiced agriculture, especially corn-growing; others were primarily hunters or fishermen. Some were largely nomadic; others had more or less settled places of residence.

12

When the earliest colonists came, the Indians were at first greatly puzzled by them, and they were not sure just how to treat them. Sometimes they were friendly to the newcomers, showing them how to grow corn, for instance; but often they were hostile. Despite the enormous difference between Indian and European culture, there was trade between the two kinds of people from their earliest contact. The Indians were eager to get iron pots, fish hooks, beads, cloth, and other articles the whites could offer in trade; later, firearms and whiskey came to be major articles of trade. The settlers, in exchange, received furs (both for their own use and for shipment back to the mother country), as well as food and other desired products. The possession of firearms and the desire to obtain furs for trade were elements which further modified Indian culture and put new pressures on their natural environment, not without repercussions for the future.

The contrast in cultures was especially sharp in the attitude toward land. The Indian concept of land ownership was entirely different from that of the whites, and the two sides never really understood each other on this point. Indians regarded land as something to be used and enjoyed, even to be defended against trespassers, but not to be owned individually, nor ever to be bought and sold in the commercial sense. One tribe might be driven away from its ancestral hunting ground by war with another tribe, but the lost land was still claimed in some sentimental sense. When the white man sought to buy land from Indians, the latter might agree and accept a purchase price or a gift, yet simply not understand what the white man meant. Trouble and conflicts arose when the white man sought to exclude the Indian from the land he had bought. It was not merely that white men drove hard bargains or that Indians reneged on bargains accepted, though there was some or each; more important, there was never any real meeting of minds.

Sometimes it was individuals who sought to buy land from Indians. Later, some colonies, and the United States, entered

13

into treaties with Indian tribes over land, assuming that the tribes were independent nations. All along, individual settlers continued to invade Indian territory, in violation of treaties and agreements. Gradually, most Indian tribes were displaced westward and ultimately settled in reservations mostly in the western half of the continent. It is futile to pass judgment on this process and the methods by which it was achieved in an age which had not yet developed the humanitarian concepts which we now take for granted in free societies.

LAND, PEOPLE, CAPITAL

The classical combination of land, labor, and capital took on rather unusual forms in the early history of North America. Not only was capital scarce, which was true also in the old countries, but the proportions between labor and land were reversed. Raw land was superabundant, but labor to cultivate this dormant wealth was very scarce. The attitudes toward land could not escape being influenced by this. The sense of freedom was enhanced when the open frontier acted as a "safety valve" against possible oppressive tendencies of the rich toward the poor.

Land in North America was claimed by various European countries—more precisely, usually by the king or crown in those countries. Wars and treaties led to the drawing of boundaries between the territories so claimed, rather independently of the degree of effective control in relation to the Indians. The crown in turn conveyed land to settlers, but by different routes. For Massachusetts, Rhode Island, and Connecticut the crown gave grants of land to companies formed to promote settlement, who parceled it out among their members in various ways. New York, after it was taken from the Dutch, and Virginia (some years after first settlement) were considered as crown colonies, and rights to land generally derived from the crown at first hand; subsequently, many owners sold land to settlers. The other original colonies were generally "proprietor colonies":

a man or a group was given a very extensive area of land—a whole modern state or more—to govern and to dispose of to settlers, subject to some controls from the crown.

There were efforts, mostly unsuccessful, by both crown and proprietors, to make land high-priced, either when sold or when rented to settlers. The motive of financial gain was important to some, less so to others. Some had extravagant and unwarranted expectations of gain; others were more realistic. In fact, land could not command a high price, either for sale or for rent; there was simply too much of it, and too few settlers. Settlers refused to pay high prices or rents and nominal land-owners were unable to collect them. The cost of making a farm out of the forest was high in real terms—that is, in terms of labor used, if not in money invested. The kind of farming that was possible in many areas did not provide much cash out of which to pay for land. With vast areas of land awaiting settlement and development, settlers saw no reason why they should pay high prices for any specific tract. Land did have value, it was highly prized and much sought after, and it was the subject of many transactions and much bargaining; but there was a persistent tendency to keep its money price low. These attitudes toward the price of land, built up in the early colonial days, persisted through the whole era of land disposal, and they still leave their mark. Most important, the situation of abundance of land and scarcity of labor gave the logical basis for a land system dominated by full individual ownership.

During the whole period of early settlement, throughout the colonial period and long thereafter, there was a great shortage of labor. Most colonists obtained some land of their own on which they produced principally what they needed for themselves, selling little. Their standard of living was governed largely by the productivity of their land and their labor. Those who sought to produce export crops had considerable difficulty in finding workers. One method was to bring indentured servants from England—persons who agreed to work for a period of years (usually seven) without wages as a means of repaying the cost of passage to the New World. Various other measures were also taken to encourage immigration. Part of the solution was to use slaves—men and women bought or captured along the coast of Africa. Their effect upon agriculture and upon society was considerable, mainly in the southeastern states where they came to be a large part of the work force.

With the simple tools of those days, the productivity of labor was low by modern standards. Output per man—whether self-employed, indentured, or slave—was low and provided only small amounts for commercial exchange. The indentured servant who received food and shelter but no wages was not so much worse off than the free working man as one might expect. Yet the abundance of the land made for a level of living which compares favorably with that of many underdeveloped countries today. No careful comparison has been made between living levels in Europe and America at that time. There is no doubt that the settlers generally were upgraded socially, and the much higher rate of population increase in America than in Europe, without any concomitant fall in *per caput* income, is one index of relative well-being by the conditions of the epoch.

Capital was more scarce in America than in Europe, and the cost of importing tools and other necessities was high. Local manufacture gradually developed, earliest in New England where conditions for agriculture were the least favorable. The colonies depended upon the old continent for supply of capital, not only until the Revolutionary War, but also throughout the nineteenth century.

GOLD, TOBACCO, AND EXPORTS

Strong as was the appeal of vacant land, several promoters of colonies, and many colonists too, had hopes of getting rich quickly by other means than by tilling their own soil. This attitude had dominated the Spanish exploration and conquest of

16

the lands farther south, and it left its mark also on the North American colonies along the Atlantic Coast. It was to be a strong force in the exploration and exploitation of lands farther west in the United States. Gold has always been able to attract adventuresome people. The Spaniards struck it rich, initially, in Peru where they robbed the natives of the accumulations of centuries. They searched elsewhere, too, usually with scant success. English and other explorers along the Atlantic Coast sought gold, too. Fortunately for the development of the country, they found almost none.

Others wanted land to produce export crops out of which to make a fortune. Tobacco was the great success crop for this purpose. Its export to England paid for return cargoes of many kinds. Other export crops, such as indigo, were tried, especially in the South, sometimes meeting with limited success for periods of time. Much later, after the colonial period, cotton became the great export crop of the South. The desire to grow export crops fueled the efforts to import labor, including slaves, and was the basis for the plantation system of agriculture. So great was the emphasis on export crops that a Virginia governor in the early years saw fit to require a defined production of corn as a condition for growing tobacco, for fear that the settlers might starve if food shipments from outside went astray or were delayed.

Farther north, agriculture was more directed to subsistence production and less toward export. New England exported fish and started early to develop handicrafts and some industry with a certain amount of sales to markets elsewhere. Other earnings to pay for imports came from commerce based on sailing ships built in the area.

During the entire colonial period, the economy of North America was "land based" in an extreme degree. Most of the people practiced some agriculture, and the towns were mainly commercial and service centers for surrounding agricultural areas. In the next chapter we shall examine more closely the systems of land use and land tenure in the colonial period.

17

CHAPTER 3

Land Use and Land Tenure in the Colonial Period

The colonial period is almost half of the history of North America. From the first settlement in Jamestown in 1607 until the Declaration of Independence in 1776 is nearly one hundred and seventy years; from the adoption of the Constitution in 1788 to the mid-1960's is little more than one hundred and seventy years. During the long colonial period the population was small, the economy weak. But these years were in many ways formative, and much of the following history of the United States has been influenced by this early development. Foremost among these influences is the character which the early pioneers had to develop. Resourcefulness and independence were necessary to succeed in frontier settlement; the weak and the incompetent were automatically weeded out. The frontiersman became oriented toward the immediately practical, often a little suspicious of theory and ideas, and somewhat ingrown in his outlook on life. These attitudes carried over into all phases of economic, social, and political life. For a long time, America drew on Europe for ideas and inventions no less than for capital, and the expanding settlements were busy enough just to implement and to manipulate without having to delve into the bases of knowledge.

The colonial influence was, of course, especially profound on the systems of land use and land tenure. In this chapter we shall sketch briefly the outstanding characteristics of these systems in the colonial period. How formative this early experience was should become evident in following chapters.

18

LAND SETTLEMENT PATTERNS

The way colonists arranged their settlements depended on several factors, such as their ideals and goals, the relation between population numbers and land area (see Chapter 2), and the political organization of the colony governments. Nearly all the early colonists were farmers, during at least part of their lives or part of each year, and the need to farm to make a living dominated the settlement pattern.

In the New England colonies, a group of settlers obtained permission, from the king in the first case and from the colony government later, to form a new settlement. Their request was investigated as far as circumstances would permit—in particular with regard to the suitability of the area chosen for settle-

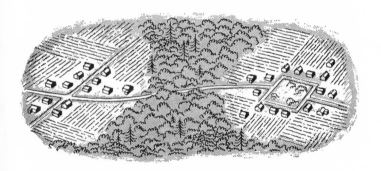

FIG. 1—NEW ENGLAND SETTLEMENT PATTERNS

New England villages in colonial times were planned and developed as units. Houses were grouped along roads or around village greens, with fields stretching away from the village toward the forests. Lands were surveyed and land records kept.

ment and the competence of the leadership group. After obtaining permission, the initial settlers moved as a group and established a new town. They surveyed the lands allotted to them and maintained title records on those lands. The village was laid out, often with a small common grazing and meeting ground in the center, with houses and big yards for gardens clustered around. The settlers worked together to clear the first fields, which were divided among them all. Fields cleared later were divided similarly. The settlement expanded as a whole, and each family received a share in both the better and the poorer land. Livestock was often herded in common on the uncleared land of the village.

This settlement pattern had several advantages. Land titles were clear, land speculation was at a minimum, and agricultural development of the whole village proceeded apace. The settlers learned to work together and to govern themselves efficiently by democratic means. Settlements were typically of a single religious denomination; religious intolerance was still strong.

In the southern colonies, extensive use was made of the idea of "headrights." As originally conceived, this system was not unlike the homestead law of more than two hundred years later. Each man who came to the new colonies was given, as a headright, a tract of land, usually 50 acres, on which he was expected to make a living. Soon, however, people who brought in new immigrants were given headrights for these. The ship's captain, the planter who paid the fare, and the indentured servant each received a headright on the latter's entry into the colony. Still later, headrights were sold for cash, and some were given fraudulently. People who received headrights could select them where they chose among land not yet occupied by other individuals. They were supposed to have the land surveyed and the deed recorded; but, in practice, surveys were often inaccurate and the records of poor quality. There were many cases where two or more men claimed the same land, and disjointed small pieces of land often occurred between larger surveyed tracts. Speculation in land was very common; it was a typical way to acquire a fortune. Many settled their land, if at all,

20

under arrangements individually made, and each man tried to select the best possible land for himself. Purchase of headrights formed one major basis for the large plantations which gradually developed in the southern colonies.

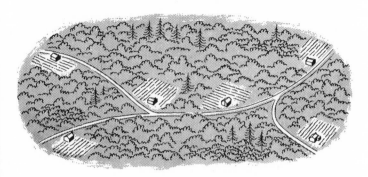

FIG. 2—SOUTHERN SETTLEMENT PATTERNS

In the South, most colonial land settlement was an individual affair. Farms were scattered through the woods. Land surveys were often poor and land title records not clear. As a result, many small and irregular shaped pieces of land sometimes lay unclaimed between farms, and disputes over farm boundaries and land titles were common.

In New England, the method of colonization and the subsistence character of agriculture worked together to develop a system of rather small farms, each occupied and operated by its owner. Small farms predominated also in the Middle Atlantic colonies, in spite of some rather large landholdings. Even in the southern colonies the small owner-operated farms greatly outnumbered the plantations, but the latter gave many of the dominant characteristics to the agriculture, the economy, the social life, and the political structure of these colonies.

The methods of land transfer just described were those most common in the colonial period. Many other methods were also in use. Title could pass directly from the crown to a landholder,

21

but usually it went through the colonial government, whether proprietary or group settlement. Land was also granted to men for military service, especially against the Indians; some land was sold directly for cash; and numerous other devices were used at one time or another.

AGRICULTURAL DEVELOPMENT

The development of agriculture in the colonies had a slow start. Even in England in the early seventeenth century, agriculture was still mainly of medieval type. The problems posed by the new country were serious. The crops which the settlers brought over from England were not well adapted to the heavily forested country. Slowly, settlers learned to grow crops native to America, using methods developed by the Indians over long periods of time.

The earliest settlements often took advantage of open lands, some of which were abandoned Indian cornfields. Soon, however, the colonists had to begin clearing the forest. We mentioned above (in Chapter 2) the primitive methods by which this was usually done. Before the dead tree stumps and roots had rotted away, farming had to be by small plots between these obstacles. Plows and draft animals were scarce but they would often have been useless on this type of farm land. Even hand tools were often in very scarce supply. In the new clearings, settlers learned to dig small holes with shovels or spades, and plant corn or some other crop this way. Only much later, as fields were better cleared and plows were more common, did it become practical to grow wheat and other English crops requiring broadcast sowing.

The early colonists had particular difficulties with livestock. The long ocean voyage was expensive and livestock losses were high, so that the purchase of animals in the colonies required more money than most settlers could afford. The animals imported often died, especially during the winter, partly because

22

the colonists underestimated the severity of the winters and partly because they lacked good hay and other livestock feed. It took some time before the earliest settlements acquired any horses or cattle, and many years before each farmer had his own. The settlements lacked good fences, and the Indians frequently sought to drive off and kill the cattle for meat. Cattle and horses could be herded, but pigs presented a special problem. The pig can go semiwild very quickly, foraging for itself and destroying crops and gardens, while evading capture with a surprising degree of cunning and agility.

Gradually the settlements made agricultural progress in several directions. More land was cleared, and that already cleared was freed of stones, stumps, and roots. Gradually more tools and simple machines were acquired, with rising productivity as a consequence. Through gradual adaptation to the environment, better methods were devised of growing crops as well as of harvesting and storing them. Livestock gradually multiplied in numbers and improved in quality. In New England, agriculture continued on the whole to be subsistence farming, while other activities supplied what cash was needed. There were some exceptions; the Connecticut Valley became the first wheat belt of the North American colonies, for instance, selling its wheat in other areas. New England also gradually developed fishing, forest industries, and above all trade as a major part of its economic base.

Farther south, in the Middle Atlantic colonies and in the southern ones, agriculture was basic not only to the colonists' needs but also for export. We have already mentioned the role of tobacco; exports were roughly a million pounds annually twenty to thirty years after the first settlements began, but by the Revolution they had reached 100 million pounds of tobacco annually. This was the basis of agriculture, trade, and government in Virginia, and later in Maryland. Other crops, such as indigo and rice, were important export articles at various times. Cotton was not important until well after the Revolution. Hemp and flax were grown for domestic use but not for export. Repeated but unsuccessful attempts were made to produce silk.

TRADE

Trade was so important in the colonies, especially in New England, and its effects upon the whole life of the colonies was so great, that it must be briefly mentioned even in a discussion of land use and land tenure. It had important effects upon them, too.

New England was not well adapted to agriculture, and in particular it did not produce much that could be exported. Some horses and salted meat were exported to the West Indies, as well as fish and timber. The region had excellent harbors, good and easily accessible forests, and a working force that soon learned to build excellent sailing ships. Trade was carried on along the coast with the other colonies and across the ocean with Europe. The most famous part of New England trade was a triangular system involving the West Indies and Africa. Molasses, sugar, and tobacco were brought home from the West Indies; rum was made of the molasses; the rum was taken to Africa and traded for slaves; these were transported to the West Indies and sold there. Many an early New England fortune was founded by this trade.

The Middle Atlantic colonies developed exports of furs, wheat, and other commodities; their industry and their trading fleets were not as extensive as those of New England. The southern colonies developed the export crops we have already mentioned.

Trade in colonial products and by colonial traders was regulated by numerous restrictive laws enacted and enforced by the English. Trade with England was carried largely on English ships. Many products had to be shipped first to England, then later shipped from there to European continental markets, sometimes paying double duty in the process. There was also a shortage of currency, and trade often had to be by barter or other special arrangements.

Despite all these difficulties, trade to and from the colonies and by colonial traders increased and flourished. It was a major factor in the economy of the colonies, and it supplied the basis of naval power in the Revolution. Trade provided an outlet for the rich surplus capacity of North American land and thus enabled domestic capital to be built up much more quickly than would have been possible in an isolated development. For the development of the tenure system, the type of trade had some significance in that it favored plantations more in areas specializing in the export of farm products than in those of a varied economic setup.

LAND TENURE IN THE COLONIES

During the colonial period, many important features of the later land tenure system took shape. The right of governments to regulate certain aspects of land tenure became firmly established. For instance, the right of government to impose land taxes, to take privately owned land for a public purpose upon payment of proper compensation, to enact laws regarding fencing, hunting and fishing, and on inheritance of landed property—all this was well established by the end of the colonial period. At the same time the right of a landowner to sell to whom he wished gradually was established and was also well recognized by the end of the colonial period. The right to bequeath land as one might choose was also established and recognized. When no will was left, laws gradually came to require equal inheritance among children or at least some part of it to go to each child. This replaced the English system of restricted inheritance. Various legal devices, known as "entails" in England and elsewhere in Europe, had enabled a landowner to assure that an estate would be kept intact and handed down to heirs of his choosing, even more than one generation later. In

25

most of the colonies, entails were gradually abolished, in others they were made conditional rather than perpetual.

In most parts of the colonies, settlers had at first been required to pay "quitrents." These were rents, payable in cash or in produce, not on the basis of any lease agreement, but in perpetual recognition of the colony's superior ownership. They represented a vestige of European institutions which originally had been a substitute for the service (of one kind or another) which a vassal had owed to his lord, in the feudal land tenure system. They were thus not a feudal institution in themselves, only a vestige of one. Although they were supposed to be paid forever, by the terms of the land grants to the settlers, many settlers resisted paying them. As time went on, quitrents were reduced in amounts or abolished entirely, sometimes only after long legislative struggles and extended delinquency on the part of the landholders. Some quitrents still remained at the time of the Revolution, but most of them were abolished by the colonial legislatures during that period. Remnants still exist, mainly in Pennsylvania and Maryland.

Land surveys and land titles, seriously inaccurate and deficient in the early settlement years in most colonies, gradually were improved. As cleared land became more valuable, the need for and the importance of better land records was more evident. It was also easier to make accurate surveys in fully settled areas with no frontier fighting against the Indians.

Comparatively little land was leased during the colonial period. Men who could undertake a lease could usually also undertake to buy land, which most of them preferred to do. The demand for leasehold farms was thus not strong. Yet some leasing did occur. As the old colonies became more fully settled and as farming became more efficient, more and more landowners sought to lease their lands, and they also found more farmers who would want to obtain land under lease. Tenancy thus became moderately common by the time of the Revolution.

26

Land tenure terms were highly variable during the colonial period, both as between colonies and areas and over time. It is safe to generalize by saying that the trend was toward giving the landowner the right to use his land as he saw fit. The idea of unrestricted land ownership, in contrast to feudal and post-feudal European land tenure, was widely held by the time of the Revolution, and it was to dominate American land history for a century or more afterward. This trend runs parallel with similar, if slower, tendencies in Europe during the same epochs.

THE REVOLUTION AND LAND HISTORY

At the time of the Revolution, the colonies had reached a fairly high level of economic development, by the standards of those times. Their population was still small—somewhat more than 3 million, but increasing rapidly, and the perspicacious could already anticipate the day when these English colonies would have more people than Old England. The first census (1790) enumerated close to 4 million people; the second one (1800), over 5 million. Ninety percent of this population were farmers or those otherwise closely tied to the land. Measured with the yardstick of an age which knew nothing of many amenities which the twentieth century takes for granted, Americans of the late eighteenth century were well off. Farms in the older settled areas were often quite productive and relatively prosperous, those along the frontier were less so. The land owner had a large measure of security, both legal and economic, and a large measure of independence and a reasonable hope of obtaining still better conditions as time went on.

In the seacoast towns there was a small, relatively wealthy class, mostly merchants, who lived in well-built houses, had elegant furniture, and enjoyed many of the luxuries of the day such as imported wines. Land speculation and trade with agricultural producers were the main sources of urban wealth. The larger towns had printing presses, newspapers, and many other attributes of modern urban life.

The American Revolution was a social as well as a political upheaval. In retrospect it is often overlooked that there were many colonists who were loyal to the King of England and struggled against those who wanted independence. There was an even more numerous group of colonists who largely stayed out of the struggle. Agriculture and trade went on nearly as before in most parts of the colonies. The active revolutionists were clearly a minority. The struggle went on for seven years, and, when it was won for independence, this was due in some degree to help from France and to English involvement in contemporary European affairs. The most important factor was, of course, the skillful and stubborn effort of the revolting colonists. With the winning of independence, those groups who had fought for it, and the ideals and attitudes they held, became more dominant in the life of the nation.

Some specific consequences for the land system flowed rather immediately out of the victory. The estates of "Tories" (higher-class people who had been on the side of England) were confiscated, subdivided, and sold to farmers, to help raise money to repay the costs of the war. Some, but by no means all, large landowners had been Tories, and subdivision of their estates meant a further strengthening of the class of landowning farmers. As we have already noted, quitrents and certain restrictions on land inheritance were usually abolished, thus moving further into the direction of freedom in land ownership. During and after the war, grants of land were made to soldiers as a reward for their military service. In many cases, these soldiers sold their land rights, thus setting the stage for extensive land speculation and for the accumulation of new large landholdings.

The Revolution had indirect consequences for the land system which were greater and more enduring than those just mentioned. The whole pattern of public land ownership and

28

disposal, and of private ownership and use, which will be described in more detail in the following chapters, grew naturally and more or less inevitably out of the attitudes toward land that had evolved during the colonial period and which were strengthened, even solidified, as a result of the Revolution.

CHAPTER 4

Exploration of a Continent

In all parts of the New World, exploration preceded settlement and permanent colonization. The first explorers were looking for new lands to claim for their sovereign, or for booty, or for adventure, or maybe for all three. Sometimes they were looking for suitable sites for permanent settlement. Whatever their motives, the first visitors usually did not stay very long but carried home tales to inspire others to exploration and colonization.

Long before colonization, early European explorers had sailed along the Atlantic Coast and up some of the navigable rivers. Among the English, Cabot and Hudson are memorable. French expeditions sailed up the Saint Lawrence River, explored the Great Lakes, and went down the Mississippi. These were the forerunners of the later permanent settlements of Europeans along the Atlantic Coast and on the Gulf of Mexico, which in turn evolved into the nation which exists today. A period of "taking cognizance" was indispensable before the wilderness could be approached, let alone be mastered, and thus also a necessary preparation to both land use and land tenure systems.

The Spaniards had penetrated into the Southwest still earlier, and also set foot in Florida. Their effect upon the history of North America, paradoxically, came much later and was much less incisive than that of the explorers and colonizers from northwestern Europe.

AFTER COLONIZATION

After the permanent colonies were established, exploration continued on an accelerating scale. Most of the earliest explorations had been by water. The difficulties, and the cost, of mounting a long expedition far from home base had always been a limiting factor. Exploration after colonization of the eastern seaboard continued by water, from bases in Europe or in the colonies; from the latter, expeditions by land also became of importance. As soon as the colonies were firmly established, there was a good deal of informal and unofficial exploration of both adjacent and distant lands, usually to the westward of the coastal settlements. Bands of men traveled into the new territory, either intent upon trapping and fur trading, or looking for likely future settlement locations, or just looking for adventure. Many of these explorations were never recorded in written history. Most of them were probably short, but some were certainly long both in miles and in time. Daniel Boone's adventures in Kentucky are among the most famous of these expeditions; they become spun over with legend, but there is a solid core of important facts inside these epical accounts.

Much later, and especially after the new nation was formed, the official exploration mission became a much larger factor. The Louisiana Purchase stimulated great curiosity about the new territory. The Lewis and Clark expedition penetrated the northern Rocky Mountains and continued through to the Pacific Coast. Later several others, among which Pike, Long, and Fremont, led expeditions to or through the Rocky Mountains. These official expeditions usually resulted in more or less scientific reports of varying length and quality. Today these reports are museum pieces, but at the time they exerted great influence. Such explorations continued well into the nineteenth century, to some extent even after the Civil War; among these late expeditions was that of Powell along the Colorado River.

There was also continued exploration along the Pacific Coast, after the permanent colonies had been established along the Atlantic Coast; but exploration and settlement on the Pacific proceeded independently until well after the Revolution. The Spaniards and their descendants continued exploration

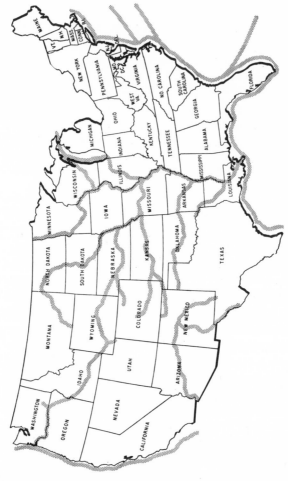

Fig. 3—EARLY EXPLORATION ROUTES

By 1700 the major coast lines and waterways had been explored, some several times, and a few notable land explorations had been carried out. In the next 150 years, major land explorations penetrated most of the West. On the scale of this map, we can show only some of the most common routes.

and settlement in the Southwest, especially California; the English explored along the Pacific Coast; and the Russians established permanent settlements in Alaska and as far down the coast as northern California.

These explorations are romantic and exciting to read about; the accounts are often stirring, even when prosaically written. What they meant to those who participated is often difficult to imagine for a modern reader. They were often genuinely valuable, both in providing more accurate information about little-known regions and in exploding myths about them. Some of the expeditions were ill-fated with death, disaster, and failure; all involved hardship and danger. We cannot here describe any of these events in detail. We can only recognize that many explorations did take place, and had to take place, before the vast mid-continent could be organized as a country.

PEOPLE PRECEDED GOVERNMENT

Throughout the colonial and early national history, it was normal that people preceded organized government in the lands along and beyond the frontier. There were always some frontiersmen who pushed onto land to which they had no legal right. That land might belong to other countries, or to Indians, or to the government of the colony or of the United States. In some cases there was as yet no treaty with the Indians; in other cases, the frontiersmen violated such a treaty. These bold frontiersmen sometimes went in conscious defiance of government, but more often without authority and without caring very much for the laws and strictures of a government which appeared so distant in those days of slow communication.

Such illegal entry was possible, among other things, because some uses of undeveloped land did not require that the user have title to it, as far as the economics of the situation was concerned. A trapper, for example, did not have to own the land on which he caught fur-bearing animals. He wanted to range

33

far and wide and to move on as the situation required. The same was true of other hunters, who lived much like the Indians, only in an even more isolated way. Some frontiersmen made lye by leaching the ashes from burned trees; the lye was basic to soapmaking in the settlements. These men had no desire to own land, as long as they could cut and burn the forests they found. Even the primitive agriculture of the frontier could be carried out economically on land not owned by the occupier. His cash investment in the land was nearly zero, and even the labor he invested in the land might not amount to more than he was willing to work for his living; if challenged, he might prefer to move on rather than pay anything for the right to stay on the land.

These types of illegal occupancy of land went through some interesting developments during the colonial and national history. At first they were looked upon as trespass, pure and simple —as they would have been in England and most other parts of Europe. Laws and edicts against such occupancy were handed down; sporadic efforts were made to enforce them, but against considerable odds, since such uses typically were along the distant and often unsafe frontier. Through the long history of settling a continent, these illegal settlers or users came to be tolerated, then even favored. In the early colonial days, these unauthorized land occupiers along the frontier played a valuable role, as a buffer against the Indians and often as advance warning posts. These services, plus the aura of adventure and romance they acquired, tended to make heroes out of the frontiersmen. The offense they committed in using or taking land not theirs was lightly regarded on a frontier where land was plentiful, and their disdain of government was often admired by more staid settlers.

Repeated pleas were made for special favors for the adventurers who went into new territory, preparing the development of the new areas and helping to fight the Indians. Shortly after the new nation was formed, special legislation began to be advocated to favor frontier settlers. First in special laws, and after 1840 in general laws, the virtues of the illegal occupier were placed in higher regard than his sins, and he was given preferential treatment in the disposition of public land. We shall return to this story in more detail in Chapter 7.

CONFLICTS WITH THE INDIANS

In chapter 2 we mentioned the problems the very earliest settlers encountered with the American Indians, and particularly the wide differences in concepts about land ownership. Most of the colonies experienced open warfare with the Indians during the first decades of their existence. The kind of uncontrolled and illegal entry into new territory by frontiersmen, which we have just described, almost invariably worsened the relations between white and red men. Time and again a colony, or the federal government, would make a treaty or bargain with some group of Indians, only to have some explorers or settlers violate the agreement. The Indians naturally felt betrayed and they retaliated as best they could. They went to war, raided the settlements, killing, burning, and looting; and the whites fought back in the same manner. During the colonial period, and in places still some time afterward, the contest was on relatively equal terms, but in time the sheer weight of numbers of the white population and their military equipment became too much for the Indians. In a sense this was a contest between economic and social systems; that of the colonists allowed rapid population increase, as Indian husbandry and mores would not. In spite of great bravery and in spite of occasional victories, the Indians were gradually pushed westward and later onto special reservations, most (but not all) of which are in the western states. The land they had to give up became available for white settlement and use. Without this displacement of the aboriginal population, the history of North America would have been very different from the one we know.

35

CHAPTER 5

Origins of the Public Domain

The next major part of our story relates how most of the land within the United States became the property of the federal government; that is the subject of this chapter. Thereafter, in later chapters, we will relate how the government disposed of most of it.

At the time of the American Revolution, all the colonies owned some land within their present borders. In addition, several of them claimed large land areas outside those borders. Six of the colonies—Maryland, Delaware, Pennsylvania, New Jersey, Rhode Island, and New Hampshire—claimed no land outside their modern boundaries. But Massachusetts, Connecticut, New York, Virginia, North Carolina, South Carolina, and Georgia maintained such claims. Some of these claims were very large, and they overlapped in several places. Virginia, for instance, asserted title to all land lying west and northwest from its shoreline, without any limit westward; this included most of the land that is now in the states of Ohio, Indiana, and Illinois.

A number of factors led these colonies, soon to be states, to cede their land to the common government. For one thing, the colonies without land claims insisted upon it, as a condition of their entry into the Union. These colonies feared the ultimate size and power of the colonies with land claims; they wanted a reasonable measure of equality among the various states, as to size and population. There was also a strong opinion in favor of using the revenue from land sales to repay the debts incurred in the common war effort. By ceding their claims to the new national government, the colonies also avoided the problem of deciding about conflicting land claims.

Cession of these claims began before independence had actually been achieved. In 1781, New York ceded its claim to about 200,000 acres in what is now northwestern Pennsylvania. Other colonies or states followed: Virginia in 1784, Massachusetts in 1785, Connecticut in 1786, South Carolina in 1787, North Carolina in 1790, and Georgia in 1802. Some of these states reserved certain lands for their soldiers and other citizens to settle upon. In the case of North Carolina, the reserved lands in what is now Tennessee absorbed almost all of its territorial claim. For other states, the reserved portions were smaller.

In Chapter 7, we shall describe in some detail how these and other lands were disposed of by the new federal government. At this point we should only mention that some measures for their disposal, the famous "Northwest Ordinances," were passed as early as in 1785 and 1787, while the new nation was still under the Articles of Confederation, before the Constitution was adopted. One very important provision in this early legislation was for the later creation of new states from the ceded lands. These new states were to be admitted on terms of complete equality with the older states. In this way the basis was laid for an expanding union of separate and equal states.

By these cessions of land from colonies and states, the new national government acquired title to all land outside the original thirteen colonies, except land tracts already in private ownership. Most of the land from Ohio through Illinois, and up into Michigan and Wisconsin, thus became the property of the federal government. So did the greater part of Alabama and Mississippi, and a much smaller part of Tennessee. The area thus acquired was very large, but still it was only a minor part of all land that has been in the federal domain at one time or another.

Some of the best farm lands in the United States (and the world) lie in these areas, and so do many of the large and

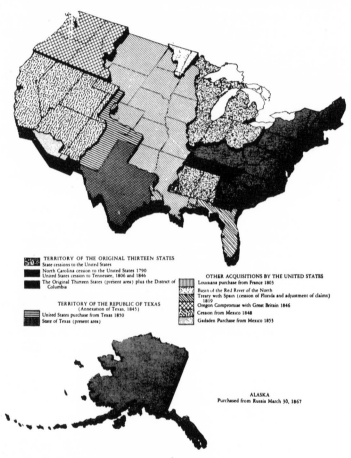

TERRITORY OF THE ORIGINAL THIRTEEN STATES
State cessions to the United States
North Carolina cession to the United States 1790
United States cession to Tennessee, 1806 and 1846
The Original Thirteen States (present area) plus the District of Columbia

OTHER ACQUISITIONS BY THE UNITED STATES
Louisiana purchase from France 1803
Basin of the Red River of the North
Treaty with Spain (cession of Florida and adjustment of claims) 1819
Oregon Compromise with Great Britain 1846
Cession from Mexico 1848
Gadsden Purchase from Mexico 1853

TERRITORY OF THE REPUBLIC OF TEXAS
(Annexation of Texas, 1845)
United States purchase from Texas 1850
State of Texas (present area)

ALASKA
Purchased from Russia March 30, 1867

FIG. 4—ACQUISITIONS

The area within the present fifty states was acquired by treaty and by purchase from various other countries.

medium-sized cities of the present age. The precedent set by federal acquisition of these lands came to dominate all the following land history of the United States.

LOUISIANA PURCHASE

A dramatic change in the extent of the United States occurred in 1803, when President Jefferson purchased the vast Louisiana Territory from France. A valuable part of that territory was the city of New Orleans and the control it gave over the traffic on the Mississippi River. This was long before the first railroads in America, and the vast inland areas depended for their development on water transportation of their products. One of the most important routes was down the Mississippi. The French colony of Louisiana had been in Spanish hands for a few decades and had just recently been taken back by France. At the time of the sale, France had its hands full of European wars, was in dire need of money, and feared that it might not be able to keep Louisiana anyway. This is why France accepted Jefferson's offer of $15,000,000. With interest, settlement of private land claims, and other costs, the total Treasury outlay ultimately reached $27 million. To modern people this does not sound very large, but for those times it was an enormous sum. On the scale of the present-day national income and federal budget, a sum of perhaps $100 billion might be comparable. Most of this land was a wilderness, very imperfectly known, and with no permanent settlers. Jefferson moved to buy this land without awaiting approval by Congress.

As a real estate deal, the Louisiana Purchase was a good bargain. Even though land was cheap in those days, the purchase price was low—about 5 cents per acre. As a political decision, the purchase was sheer genius. It almost entirely removed France from the Western Hemisphere, and it helped set the stage for the Monroe Doctrine not very many years later. Purchase of this land also greatly reduced the likelihood that any other European power might get a foothold in North America.

Out of the lands so purchased have been created all or parts of thirteen states—Louisiana, Arkansas, Missouri, Iowa, Minnesota, North Dakota, South Dakota, Nebraska, Kansas, Oklahoma, Colorado, Wyoming, and Montana. At one stroke of the pen, the total area of the United States was almost doubled. Although there were some private land claims in the territory, which usually were honored, nearly all the land became the property of the federal government, which has disposed of it in ways we shall consider in Chapter 7.

FLORIDA PURCHASE

Not many years after the Louisiana Purchase—in 1819—Spain sold to the United States what is now Florida. Spain had not been very successful in settling Florida, and it was moved by some of the same considerations that led France to sell Louisiana—fear of losing it by war, among others. The War of 1812 had demonstrated the new country's determination and ability to defend its territory. This purchase removed another foreign power from the eastern part of North America. It also removed a source of friction; border incidents had been common.

TEXAS

Texas came to the United States in a rather unusual way. It was an independent country which gave up its independence to join a larger union. Texas had been part of Mexico. Americans began settling there in modest but increasing numbers after 1821. Conflict with Mexican authorities led to armed revolt in 1836 and to independence for Texas. The new nation wanted to join the United States at once, but arguments over slavery in the Congress held up acceptance of the treaty until 1845. In the meantime, Texas was an independent republic. As such, it was able, to some extent, to negotiate about the terms on which it entered the Union. One requirement insisted upon by Texas, and accepted by the United States, was that the land within Texas, to the extent it was not already private property, should belong to the state, not to the federal government. Thus there was no federal domain in Texas, and the story of disposal of the federal domain does not apply there. However, the state government sold or gave away its lands in a manner rather similar to that followed in the public domain states.

When Texas was admitted as a state, there was some uncertainty over its boundaries, especially to the west and northwest. In 1850, the United States bought from Texas its claims to nearly 79 million acres of land, lying in the present states of New Mexico, Colorado, Kansas, Wyoming, and Oklahoma. This land then was added to the federal domain.

PACIFIC NORTHWEST

The United States and Britain each sought to obtain the Pacific Northwest, by exploration and by settlement. During the period from 1818 to 1844, there were arrangements for joint settlement and joint control. The latter became unsatisfactory to settlers from the United States, because in fact the Hudson's Bay Company largely dominated. As settlers from the United States became more numerous, they demanded that their country achieve clear title to the area. Following some acrimonious argument with Britain, a treaty was signed in 1846 which gave the United States the territory which is now the states of Washington, Oregon, and Idaho, and parts of Montana and Wyoming.

PACIFIC SOUTHWEST

The annexation of Texas in 1845 did not reconcile Mexico to its loss. In the United States, there were many who wanted to add the Pacific Southwest, and especially California, to the territory of the country. Some historians believe that the war with Mexico, in 1846, was deliberately provoked by the United States, with these territorial ambitions as a motive, since Mexico was unwilling to sell. The war ended in a decisive defeat for Mexico. The peace treaty gave the United States the area that is now the states of California, Nevada, and Utah, and large parts of Arizona, New Mexico, Colorado, and Wyoming. This land was paid for, however, at a price per acre roughly the same as had been paid for the Louisiana Territory. A few years later, in 1853, a further strip of land across southern New Mexico and Arizona was acquired from Mexico (the Gadsden Purchase).

In both the northern and southern Pacific areas, the land became the property of the federal government. A relatively few private land claims existed, which were recognized. In certain areas, including some parts of western Louisiana Territory, title problems proved complicated.

ALASKA

The last large territorial acquisition was Alaska, which was bought from Russia in 1867. As noted above, the Russians had early explored the northern Pacific Coast. Their interest was chiefly in furs. They built a few forts and semipermanent establishments, but there was virtually no agriculture, for most of the area they explored was unsuited to it. With the sea otter, a chief fur species, nearly extinct, and with other fur sources depleted, Russia was willing to sell. There was much criticism within the United States over the purchase—it was widely called "Seward's Folly," after the Secretary of State who negotiated the purchase. Today Alaska is one of the states of the Union, and the strategic importance of having no Old-World power on the North American continent is greater than ever.

The land in Alaska, except for very small private claims, became public domain. Although generally open to disposal under the various land laws, with some special laws applying only to Alaska, very little land had passed out of public ownership up to the time when the state was admitted to the Union in 1959.

OTHER AREAS

After expansion across the North American continent had been concluded, lands acquired elsewhere, by treaty or war, came in a different category. These extra-continental possessions never had a public domain in the sense that the public land laws were applicable to them. Hawaii was an independent nation which joined the United States at its own request. War with Spain brought the dependencies of Puerto Rico (now a "commonwealth") and Guam, for a long time also the Philippines (which were given their independence by treaty), for various times also Cuba. The Virgin Islands were acquired by purchase, some Pacific Islands as a consequence of World War I. The public land laws of the United States have never applied to any of these possessions.

43

CHAPTER 6

Land Survey, Titles, and Records

Dependable titles and property descriptions are basic to any system of private land ownership. How important they are can best be seen when they are absent, as in large parts of Latin America; much confusion, uncertainty, and conflict are the result. The often quoted link between private ownership and democracy is another reason to emphasize the importance of land titles in a free country. Land titles are among the things that are often taken for granted in the United States. In most cases, when someone buys a house, for instance, he assumes that the seller has clear title which he conveys to the buyer. Even in the United States, however, the system of land titles and property descriptions is sufficiently complicated so that anyone who buys valuable property should know the system, be aware of its pitfalls, and be able to use the safeguards which the system offers.

LAND SURVEY

Land in the United States has been divided into property units under several different survey systems. The most important types of description and identification of a property which came out of these survey systems are by *metes and bounds* and by *rectangular survey*. In addition, small properties (as in cities) are usually more precisely defined by *platting*.

As noted in Chapter 3 above, different systems of land survey were used in the colonies. In New England, the town boundaries were surveyed by the colony, and the farms and fields

44

within the town were surveyed by the settlers. These surveys were crude, but at least all the land was surveyed under one common system, and the boundaries of one tract coincided with the boundaries of the neighbors. In the southern colonies, each settler was allowed to select the land he wanted; he was supposed to have it surveyed and to file the survey with a public official. Sometimes he failed to have the survey made. More seriously, this system of selecting land led to gaps between the surveys, with small irregular tracts left without owners, and it often led to overlapping properties and to conflicts.

In both areas, these early surveys described properties by landmarks, natural or man-made; each property took on the shape which topography and human whim decided. This method was not very practical for a rapid settlement of vast areas. Before the new government of the United States could dispose of its lands, it had to survey them. A quick and dependable method was needed. The matter of land survey occupied the Continental Congress a good deal, and later the United States under the Articles of Confederation, and still later the Congress. Several issues were debated in those days, for the members of Congress were acutely aware of the great importance of accurate and dependable land surveys. We shall not try to trace these arguments, but we shall describe the land survey system which emerged. In some ways, it seems to have absorbed elementary ideas originating in the Old World; a connection with the Roman cadastre of antiquity is not excluded. The new system was applied, with some minor local modifications, to the public domain described in Chapter 5. Even though Texas was never part of the public domain of the United States, the same type of survey system was applied there, too. A similar system has also been used in large parts of Canada, especially its western provinces.

The dominant land survey system is that of rectangular survey. A starting point for an area as large as a state or larger is chosen, often on the top of a prominent hill. This point is carefully marked. Through this point is run a north-south line, called the principal meridian, and another line is run east and west, called the base line. Parallel with these lines, on intervals of six miles, are established township lines, thus leading to the creation of six-mile squares called townships. These "geometrical" townships are in many areas also used as civilian communities (townships), but in principle the two concepts are separate and in some areas there are thus two kinds of townships. The geometrical townships in turn are divided into 36 sections, each one mile square, or with 640 acres in each. These in turn are divided into quarters, and often the quarters further into quarters or smaller tracts. In this system, each starting point has a name, such as Mt. Diablo base and meridian; townships are described according to their distance and direction from the starting point, such as township 2 south, range 3 west, or township 6 north, range 9 east. Within each township the sections are numbered from 1 to 36. The quarters of the section are described according to their position within the section, as NW 1/4, or SE 1/4, and similarly the quarters of the quarters are described according to their position within the quarter.

The results sound like gibberish to the layman: SE 1/4 of NW 1/4, Section 11, Township 3 north, range 5 west, Willamette base and meridian, for instance. But to anyone even moderately familiar with the rectangular land survey system, this positively identifies a 40-acre tract of land in western Oregon. No other tract in the whole United States has this description; no other description can be given to this tract. It is positive, both for this piece of land and as excluding every other piece of land.

In practical application, this system encountered many problems. First of all, Congress had specified that the lines of townships were to run true north and south, following the lines of longitude, and true east and west, following the lines of latitude, but also that the townships and sections were to be exact-

- TOWNSHIP GRID -

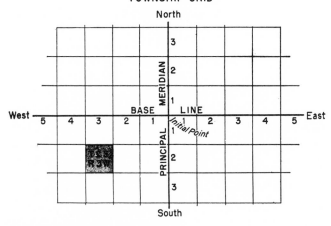

TOWNSHIP 2 SOUTH, RANGE 3 WEST

6	5	4	3	2	1
7	8	9	10	11	12
18	17	16	15	Section 14	13
19	20	21	22	23	24
30	29	28	27	26	25
31	32	33	34	35	36

SECTION 14

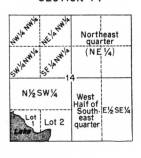

FIG. 5—GENERALIZED DIAGRAM OF THE RECTANGULAR
SYSTEM OF SURVEYS

A basic feature of the rectangular system of land surveys is an "initial point." Through this is run a "base line," from east to west, and a "principal meridian," from north to south. Ranges are measured east and west, and townships north and south. Thus the shaded block in the upper diagram is Township 2 South, Range 3 West—or T. 2 S., R. 3 W., for short. This township is six miles on a side, or contains 36 square miles. It is subdivided into 36 "sections" containing one square mile or 640 acres each, as shown in the lower left diagram. The section may be further subdivided as shown in the lower right diagram.

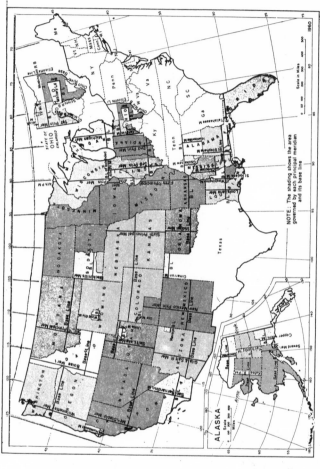

FIG. 6—PRINCIPAL MERIDIANS OF THE FEDERAL SYSTEM OF RECTANGULAR SURVEYS

All land within each shaded area can be readily and simply described in relation to the "initial point" through which the respective "principal meridian" runs. The most important item in any legal description of land is the base and meridian within which the rest of the description falls. Not all of the western United States and little of Alaska has been surveyed.

ly square. This is impossible, since the earth is round, and longitude lines converge as one goes northward. In practice this problem was met by having the township lines run as specified, with most sections exactly square, but all the adjustments thrown into the line of sections across the north and along the west of each township. To achieve larger adjustments between principal meridians and base lines, "correction lines" were introduced at certain intervals.

Other and more serious operating problems arose as this survey system was applied. Survey should have preceded settlement, but this could not always be done, as some areas received their first settlers before they had been formally acquired from the Indians. Many surveys were crudely done, with many errors; some were fraudulent, and others suspected of being so but never discarded. Section and township corners were supposed to be marked permanently, but in many cases the materials used for markers rotted away soon. Surveys were performed by private contractors until 1910, after which they were taken over by government engineers. Better equipment and more permanent metal markers make modern surveys much more dependable than the old ones.

In spite of some deficiencies, the survey system under which the public domain was conveyed to private ownership is one of the best in the world. It is intimately connected with the whole system of private land ownership in the United States.

A LASTING MARK

The original land survey has left an indelible mark upon those parts of the United States and Canada to which it was applied. The United States is a "rectangular" country, where political and civilian as well as property divisions are in squares and oblongs like a haphazard checkerboard, with most lines running directly north-south and east-west. A traveler by road or by train may notice some of these features in the Middle

49

West or on the Great Plains, but they are much more obvious from the air. The mile squares are clearly discernible, often with a road on each side; sometimes the square is clearly broken into halves, quarters, or some other fraction; sometimes property units integrate fractions of different original squares, breaking the regular pattern. Occasionally, one can also see a slight jog in a section line, which is then likely to be a township line in which a correction was made because of the curvature of the earth.

The mark left by the original land survey was even more pervasive than can be seen now. Roads typically follow the east-west and north-south section lines, even though this means going up and down hills rather than around them. Farmers tend to lay out their fields parallel to the boundaries of their land, even though this may mean cultivating up and down rather than around the slope. Much erosion has been caused or accelerated in this way. Some land experts, observing these types of destructive land use, have been highly critical of the rectangular land survey. With the knowledge that comes with hindsight, today we can point out ways in which the rolling prairie or forest areas might have been subdivided more along natural drainage lines, thus promoting better land use. But at the time when the lands were first surveyed, no one had the necessary knowledge to do this, and the nation was moving westwards too fast to await the slow process of trial and error by which land division and settlement had been decided in the Old World as well as along the eastern seaboard of the United States.

Modifications in the original checkerboard pattern come gradually. Districts for drainage and watershed control have to follow natural units, for instance. Many of the new interstate highways are laid out diagonally across the rectangular system rather than running north-south or east-west; and farmers sooner or later re-group the triangular land parcels along such highways, integrating them with farms most suitable to receive such parcels. When larger farm units are built up, e.g., on the

50

Great Plains, land parcels are often grouped together that will allow contour plowing even across section lines.

But these changes do not do away with the rectangular system as a way of identifying land parcels. A property composed of fragments of several rectangular sections can still be described accurately by describing each of the component parcels. The advantages of a single, positive system of identification and description for each tract of land are very great indeed. The future will be one of gradually adjusting to the needs of rational land use, while still using the original grid as an instrument of identification and description.

The area identified and described within the rectangular survey system is often somewhat imprecise. Farm land sales instruments often say, for example, "80 acres, more or less," implying that the sale regards the parcel as described but without guaranteeing any exact area figure. When land is subdivided into very small parcels, as in urban areas, rural residences, service stations, industrial building lots in rural areas, etc., then it is often necessary to measure the parcel with modern instruments and establish its boundaries and its surface size with more accuracy than would follow from successive subdivision of the imprecisely measured parcels that resulted from the rectangular survey. The precision map thus established is called a "plat," and the procedure is termed "platting." In several states, platting is mandatory whenever land is subdivided in a way that creates parcels below a certain stated minimum size.

LAND RECORDS

Not only must land be surveyed, but an adequate system of land records must be kept. The federal government kept land records for the public domain, until each piece of property went into private ownership. The early records look strange to a modern reader, but they served the purpose well. The land titles of more than half of all privately owned land in the United

States trace back to these records. Even today, it is sometimes necessary to go back to those early records, to be sure that a piece of land actually is in private ownership. Sometimes flaws in title are discovered, and rather complicated legal procedures are necessary to cure such flaws. Most land records are kept in county offices. Land titles are recorded there, and each change in title is also recorded. The public servants who keep these records are not conspicuous to the general public, but the work they do is very important to the society and its economic system.

When a piece of property is sold, the buyer or his attorney usually asks an expert on land titles, or "title abstracter," to "search" the title; the attorney then examines the evidence looking for possible flaws. Ordinarily, he assures the buyer that the title is perfect, in return for a fee. This means that he pledges to defend the title in court should the need arise. Sometimes a search is made through county and other records to be sure that there is a clear line of title from the first holder right down to the seller in the case at hand. In this process, the records are subjected to thorough checks and double checks, so that errors are sooner or later ferreted out. Many of the flaws that are discovered are quite unimportant—a man transferred a property to a son without proper legal papers, and the like.

Throughout the history of the United States, disputes over land titles have been taken to the courts for settlement. Naturally, this too has its difficulties. Lawsuits often cost so much that they are not very practical for poor men. Yet on the whole the courts have operated to make land titles secure.

Today, it is very rare that a person who follows accepted procedures loses property because of defective land title. In some cases and in some areas, old claims may be extinguished by prescription, thus protecting recent buyers against the risks of long forgotten flaws. More important is a widespread system of "title insurance," available in most but not in all states, through which certain insurance companies guarantee property owners from losses in case title flaws were to come to life and prior claims be honored in court. The insurance company only guarantees the value of the property, not necessarily undisturbed possession. On the whole, the system of land titles and records works smoothly; some people think it is too costly, yet it does guarantee land titles in nearly all cases.

CHAPTER 7

Federal Land Disposal: Government Power and Private Property

Throughout the nineteenth century, disposal of the public domain was perhaps the most important single factor in the political as well as the economic life of the United States. It also became one of the basic elements in the nation's culture. Debates in Congress and political campaigns often centered around public land issues. The economic development of the country rested to a large extent on the settlement and improvement of the new lands. The frontier spirit remained a pervasive influence on the nation's life during the entire century.

When the new Union was established in 1788, it owned, or would soon own, roughly 150 million acres of land—an area about the size of Texas, or of France, for instance. By 1850, through the various land acquisitions described in Chapter 5, the total area that had at one time or another been in the public domain had risen to nearly 1,500 million acres; the maximum at one and the same time was 1,200 million. These figures should be compared with the total area of the 48 contiguous states, which is roughly 1,900 million acres. Thus, about three quarters of the total area of the continental United States has been public domain at one time or another. Through the nineteenth century, the federal government disposed of two thirds of the public domain, or about half of the contiguous area of the country.

These quantity data indicate the scope of economic opportunity that was offered, in various ways, to the daring and the

54

hardheaded. Several million people drew on this opportunity; many acquired homes for their families, and a few made fortunes. The abundance of free or cheap land was a large part of

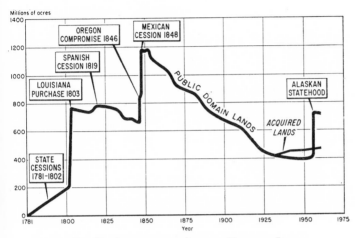

FIG. 7—APPROXIMATE AREA OF FEDERAL LANDS
IN THE UNITED STATES, 1781–1960

The area of federal land within the United States at any time is a result of the balance between land acquisition and land disposal. From 1781 to 1850, land acquisition dominated, and federal holdings reached their peak, at 1,200 million acres, in the latter year. From then until 1930, federal ownership of land declined. Since 1930, federal ownership of land has increased modestly, owing to purchases of land from private citizens. With the admission of Alaska to the Union, federal holdings within the states rose sharply; this land had previously been owned by the federal government, but Alaska was only a territory.

the attraction for immigrants from Europe. Disposal of the federal domain became one of the central themes of nineteenth century American history.

LAND SALES

With the achievement of independence, the new nation owned a great deal of land, was heavily in debt, and had a seriously depreciated currency. Everyone agreed that the publicly owned lands should be disposed of and converted to private property, but there was controversy about the means and the tempo. The two main opposing arguments were: should the public domain be sold chiefly as a means of obtaining public revenue, or should the disposal aim, above all, at settling a large class of landowning farmers? Those who placed emphasis on sales for revenue also wanted to sell large tracts to a small number of buyers; they were either not concerned with the kind of rural community that would develop, or favored a society of large landowners and tenant farmers. Alexander Hamilton is most often quoted as a spokesman for this opinion. Thomas Jefferson, by contrast, and his followers entertained a philosophy in which landowning farmers were a highly desirable social element, and they wanted above all to use the public domain to further the development of this kind of society.

At first, land sales were made principally to obtain revenue, but gradually this emphasis became weaker. In the early years there was rather little demand for the land owned by the federal government, because the states and individual speculators owned much land, often close to the settlements. Land sales, and the revenue they brought, were therefore not important in the early years of the republic. Income from land sales was less than 10 percent of the federal revenue until 1814. After that time, land began to be sold much more rapidly, and by the middle of the 1830's, land sales accounted for over 40 percent of the income of the national government. They even created, for a short time, a surplus in the federal treasury.

In the 1820's and 1830's, land sales were at the center of a strong tendency toward economic speculation. As yet there was no central banking system and individual banks could issue banknotes as they saw fit. Paper money was often at a discount, but still it could be issued freely. Its value depended ultimately on the assets backing it, and since much of it went into land speculation, the value of money could fluctuate with the prospects for continued rise in land values. A period of speculation fever (a "land boom") ended in 1837, land prices fell sharply, many people lost their paper fortunes, and the country was plunged into a major economic depression.

During the first half of the nineteenth century or a little longer, there was a continuous struggle between settlers and land speculators over the terms of federal land sales. The speculators wanted the land offered for sale in the larger cities along the Atlantic Coast, and in relatively large parcels—several thousand acres in each. The settlers wanted the land to be sold near the frontier, in units of average farm size. Each sought a low price for the land, with easy credit terms. Gradually, the methods of selling shifted in favor of the settlers. The minimum unit of sale was 640 acres in 1796 but was gradually reduced to 80 acres in 1820. Land offices were also gradually opened nearer to the land being sold. Land prices were very low by modern standards—$2 per acre or less—but these prices were higher in those days, relative to prices in general and to incomes. Various experiments were tried with credit; the results were often bad, sometimes disastrous. Agreements to pay on installment plan often ended in failure. Some land reverted to the federal government because the price had not been paid, but often a generous Congress forgave debts or extended payment periods.

During the first half of the nineteenth century, sale was almost the only way by which federal land could become private property; the principal alternative was by "land-warrant" for military service. Other methods were made available later during the century, but sales continued long after the other means had been added.

57

PRE-EMPTION

Land could be acquired by pre-emption by those who had already settled on it as pioneers. Legally these people were squatters on public property; how they should be treated was one of the major political issues during some of the formative decades of the country's history.

As we noted in Chapter 4, land settlement tended to run ahead of land survey. After survey there was also often some interval before the land became offered for sale, and settlement usually proceeded during this period too. Pioneers cleared forest, grew crops, and erected rough buildings, all without having any legal title to the land. The controversy about these people contrasted their merits as pioneers against their illegal status. As the country expanded over the vast virgin areas of the federal domain, the tendency grew stronger to give the frontier settlers favored terms. The controversy was over the right of the settlers to pre-empt the land on which they squatted, at a low price and without having to compete with other prospective buyers about that particular tract.

A series of pre-emption acts were passed, almost from the first cash sales of land, but generally they applied only to certain areas or only for limited periods of time. The several acts passed one after the other protected most settlers. In 1841, a general Pre-emption Act was passed. At that time it applied only to land which had been settled after land survey, but shortly afterwards it was amended to include settlement before survey also. When land was offered for sale, a settler had a right to buy, for $1.25 per acre, the land on which he had settled, not to exceed 160 acres. He could not do this if he already owned more than 320 acres. These acts were of great help to actual settlers, and also to small-scale speculators who could take advantage of their terms.

In practice, the pre-emption acts were much abused. Many people would file claims and assert residence when in fact they had never lived upon the land. Land acquired in this way at the low fixed price could thereafter be sold at a profit to actual settlers. "Claim clubs" were organized by people asserting claims in this way, and such clubs could sometimes force the settlers to buy land from them rather than from the federal land office. In other cases, the clubs merely protected the legitimate claims of the members.

LAND GRANTS FOR PUBLIC PURPOSES

Land was the principal kind of wealth that existed in the early and mid-nineteenth century. Federal subsidy to states and communities, for the construction of needed improvements, mainly took the form of land grants.

The first, and the most important, category of land grants was in support of public schools at the elementary grade level. In the early nineteenth century, a large part of the population was still illiterate. The demand for free public education had strong appeal in a country where the Constitution granted all men the "pursuit of happiness," but it was also a very bold idea at that time with the scarcity of resources in excess of a modest, semi-subsistence type of well-being. The Northwestern Ordinances of 1785 and 1787, passed during the Confederation period, provided that one section, or 640 acres, out of each township should be available to support local public schools. Later, this grant was raised for the states which came into the Union to two and then to four sections. Thus, 3, 6, and 11 percent, respectively, of the federal domain was granted to the states upon their admission to the Union, in support of public schools. If the sections officially named for the purpose happened already to be in private hands, the states were allowed to select other sections "in lieu."

Later many states were given other grants, known as "quantity grants" because they were for a stipulated total area rather than for certain sections in each township. These grants were

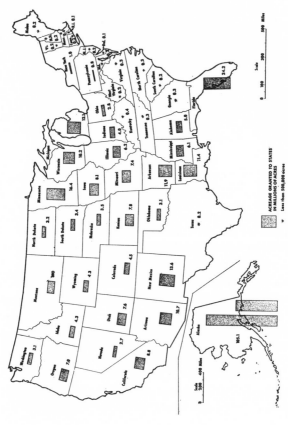

FIG. 8—FEDERAL LAND GRANTS TO STATES, 1803–1962

One major means by which land was transferred from the federal government was by grants to states. The largest were made to the states with large areas of "swamp" land within their borders, and to some of the states last admitted to the Union, which received larger common school grants. Alaska has received the largest grants of all, both in absolute area and as a proportion of its total area. Some states have retained substantial parts of the land received, but most of for the support of other public institutions. The most notable of these were for agricultural and mechanical arts colleges, which to this day are known as "land grant colleges." Other grants supported schools for the blind, mental hospitals, mining schools, and other institutions. The quantity grants were valuable also because the states were allowed to select the lands where they chose. These grants had a catalytic effect; they provided a larger public endorsement for the ideas for which they were made and a significant part of the initial costs. They also gave the states the impetus to provide the rest of the money from other sources. They were the forerunner of a very common feature of federal-state relations in modern times known as the "grants-in-aid."

Another type of land grant was of swamp and overflow lands, given to states for the purpose of land improvement. This was based on the assumption that the states would be better equipped to improve those lands than was the federal government. This assumption proved essentially mistaken. The states were in fact much less well placed to undertake the large capital expenditures needed for extensive land reclamation. A great deal of valuable cropland, subject to occasional overflow, was given to states in this way; often the states sold this land at very low prices to land speculators with political influence. Much of the Central Valley of California and the Mississippi Delta went this way. The acreages involved were substantial.

Another major type of land grant was in aid of transportation. Small grants were made for wagon roads and canals, but large ones were made for railroads. The railroad grants began in 1850 and were largely completed by 1870. The typical grant to aid in railroad construction consisted of alternate sections of land for a specified distance on either side of the rail line. The minimum price at which the remaining sections were offered for sale (which meant also their fixed price at pre-emption sale) was then doubled, both to provide the government with as much revenue as it would otherwise have received, and to

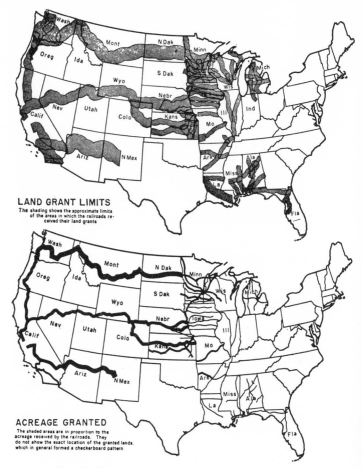

FIG. 9—FEDERAL LAND GRANTS FOR RAILROADS

The land grants to railroads were ordinarily for alternate sections. The outer limits of the grant areas were relatively wide, partly because much of the land within them was already in private ownership and the railroads were able to select only the open public domain. The areas actually granted, while substantial, were only a small portion of the total area within grant limits.

reflect the fact that these lands were more valuable once the railroads were built. This, of course, also helped the railroads obtain favorable prices when they sold the land. If the land granted on the basis of the above mentioned principle happened to be already in private ownership, then "in lieu" lands could be selected, often within a specified further distance from the rail line. Many railroads sold their lands as fast as they could; others held large acreages for comparatively long periods. In return for the grant, the federal government obtained special rates on its freight shipped over these rail lines.

This concession was not repealed until 1940 and 1945; it has been calculated that it brought the federal government something in excess of $1,000 million in reduced freight rates. There has been much discussion as to who gained most from these land grants—the railroads or the federal government. If the "multiplier effect" is considered, then of course no distinct answer can be given. At any rate, these grants have contributed to the economic development of the country, and they were an important method of transfer of federal land into private ownership.

THE HOMESTEAD ACT AND
ITS SUCCESSORS

The agitation over land for settlers was no by means ended with the passage of the Pre-emption Act in 1841. The ultimate goal of those favoring the cause of individual settlers was to grant virgin land, free of charge, to people who would cultivate it on family-scale farms. The social ideal embodied in such a goal brought conflict with the southern plantation owners and their political interest as they saw it. The slavery states feared that in the future they would be outvoted by the nonslavery states. Southern politicians therefore favored a system of land holdings which would entail the extension of the slavery system to about half of the new states to be formed out of the federal domain. Efforts to pass a homestead law, granting free land to settlers, were therefore defeated up until the outbreak of the Civil War.

The Homestead Act was finally passed in 1862, with the southern states out of Congress. It did not replace the land disposal system that had operated until then; it simply added another mode of land disposal to the existing ones. The new rule was radical in form but had limited effect. Under the Homestead Act of 1862, prospective settlers could claim a standard allotment, usually 160 acres, of federal domain land free of charge, against payment of small fees to cover administrative costs. The settler must be the head of a family, or over twenty-one years of age, and either a citizen of the United States or one who had declared his intention of becoming one, and he should either cultivate the holding for five years, or reside on it for five years, before title could pass to him. No previous "squatting" was required, and within limits, the settlers could themselves choose the land they wanted.

The Homestead Act was intended to relieve unemployment in the cities and to expand the system of family-scale, owner-operated farming. It had little effect, if any at all, for the former purpose; even for the latter, the effect was limited. At this late date, much of the best land was already in private ownership, and in the areas in which homesteading could become important, the standard allotment (of 160 acres, sometimes only 80) was often too small, on account of dry climate. The effect was further reduced because of the way the provisions of the Homestead Act could be combined with those of earlier laws, such as the Pre-emption Act of 1841. A homesteader could, after six months of occupancy, convert his homestead claim to a pre-emption claim, pay $1.25 per acre ($2.50 on 80 acre tracts in favored areas), obtain title, and then sell. Often this was abused as a disguised way for land speculators to get hold of the land. The $200 were not seldom procured through a loan from a speculator. Apart from outright fraud cases, there were many homesteaders who failed to meet the obligations of the

Homestead Act, for the simple reason that pioneer farming is a tough job and many underestimated what it would take to carve a farm out of the wilderness.

Several later laws were enacted to supplement the Homestead Act. The Timber Culture Act in 1873 provided that a person could obtain 160 acres of land if he would plant trees on 40 acres of it—later changed to 10 acres. Title could not be obtained in less than eight years, and the settler must show that 675 or more trees to the acre were still living and thriving. This act was widely misused. Under the Desert Land Act (1877), a settler could get 640 acres (later reduced to 320) if he would irrigate one-eighth of it. This act was also exploited through numerous fraudulent practices. The area that could be obtained as a homestead was increased to 320 acres in 1909 and to 640 acres in 1916, as settlement extended to drier and drier areas; and residence was reduced from five to three years in 1912. The Carey Act (1894) provided for grants to states for irrigation projects and envisaged essentially a homestead system on reclaimed lands. The federal Reclamation Act (1902) provided for federal irrigation projects. Most of the land irrigated under this act has been and is private property.

SUMMARY OF LAND DISPOSAL

Some idea of the relative importance of the various methods of land disposal can be gained from a few statistics. For the 48 contiguous states, the area in millions of acres is given as follows:

Total land area	1,904
Original public domain	1,442
Total disposition, all methods	1,031
Cash sales, and miscellaneous methods	300
Homesteads	285
Grants to states	225
Military bounties and private claims	95
Railroad grants	91
Timber culture and other related acts	35

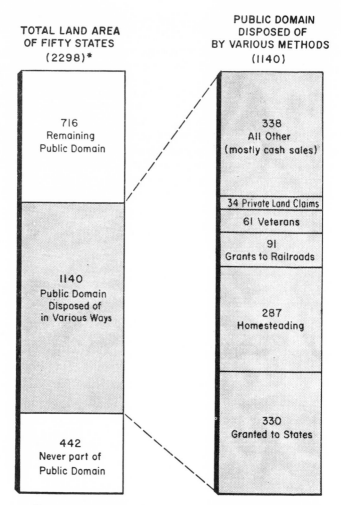

TOTAL LAND AREA
OF FIFTY STATES
(2298)*

PUBLIC DOMAIN
DISPOSED OF
BY VARIOUS METHODS
(1140)

716
Remaining
Public Domain

338
All Other
(mostly cash sales)

1140
Public Domain
Disposed of
in Various Ways

34 Private Land Claims

61 Veterans

91
Grants to Railroads

287
Homesteading

442
Never part of
Public Domain

330
Granted to States

*Figures in millions of acres.

FIG. 10—PUBLIC DOMAIN AND ITS DISPOSAL

Most land in the United States was once public domain. Half of the entire national area was once public domain but has been disposed of. States were granted a large portion of it; other large areas were sold or homesteaded, but a variety of disposal methods were employed.

These figures may be compared with the area of certain states, to indicate the scale. An average state, such as Illinois or Iowa, has a total surface of about 35 million acres; California, the second largest of the 48 states, has about 100 million acres of total area.

The area of land disposed of by a particular method is not always the best indicator of its importance. Some methods were available early, when better quality land was available; others came into operation later, when the available land was drier or generally less productive.

Some land was disposed of under mining laws. These were very important in some situations, but the total area so disposed was small relative to the areas covered by other laws. Mining laws are complex and they continue to operate at present.

ALASKA

The state of Alaska has a peculiar situation. Its total area is 365 million acres, most of which is still federal domain. From 1867 until Alaska was admitted to the Union in 1959, only about 1 million acres passed from federal to private ownership. The new state was given a very large grant, far larger than any state up to that time, which may ultimately reach 100 million acres or more; at present, the state of Alaska owns something in excess of 6 million acres, which is more than any other state owns. Most of the laws on disposal of the federal domain have been or are applicable to Alaska, and in addition some special ones have applied there only.

TRESPASS, FRAUD, SPECULATION AND WASTE

The more than a century-long disposal of the federal domain took place in a country that took shape along with this disposal. The remarkable thing is not so much that fraud, speculation, and other social disorders occurred as much as was the case, but rather that a certain modicum of order could be preserved in the process. A nation that had grown strong in fighting the wilderness favored the enterprising individual. Men with drive and stamina, or with modest capital, were striving to improve their position by getting a farm or by making money in land dealings. The land disposal process has been likened to a vast grab bag at a party, with valuable gifts for those who could get them and hold them. There were always those who shoved in ahead of others and snatched the best prizes.

As noted previously, many people occupied land without any title at all. In many cases this illegal occupancy did little damage to the land, harmed no one, and in time ended when the trespasser or someone among his successors acquired the land from the federal government. But timber trespass was a different story. This kind of trespass consisted in someone harvesting all the merchantable timber from a tract of government land and selling it for his own profit; the land was left denuded, the forest regenerated slowly if at all, and all the value of the land was gone, so that no one was interested in acquiring it. This type of trespass occurred in many parts of the country but was especially common in the Lake States; many a large fortune was made or started in this way. Grazing trespass was common throughout the West and ended only with the establishment of national forests and grazing districts, as we will discuss in Chapter 12. The productivity of range land was often impaired by uncontrolled grazing. The early mining in the West lacked any sanction in federal law; miners often established a kind of local law. When settlement ran ahead of government, people found it logical to take matters in their own hands and write their own rules.

In land acquisitions from the federal government, much outright fraud was practiced. One source of fraud was the private land claim. When the United States bought the Louisiana Purchase or other areas, or acquired territory by treaty, existing private claims were to be honored. Such claims were often difficult to prove, and this gave the opportunity for proving more than was justified. Many claims were denied, others were honored reluctantly because fraud was suspected. The settlement requirements for pre-emption and homestead rights were also often falsified; claimants would assert settlement where none existed. Respect for the government was not what it was in the Old World, and many people thought they had a right to do what they could get away with. Even when fraud was uncovered, the guilty were seldom punished seriously. Lack of manpower for law enforcement made it difficult to go after the culprits effectively.

Congress itself was rather tender in its treatment of land claimants. Many congressmen were themselves speculators or dealers in land. Many unproven and probably fraudulent private claims were verified by special congressional action. Time and again, when some group of settlers had not complied with the law, Congress would enact special legislation freeing them of their original obligation. Congress never gave the General Land Office the size and kind of staff it needed to uncover and prove fraud. The overriding interest was to get the country settled rapidly; meticulous probing of each case might have slowed the process.

Speculation in land, especially land recently sold or granted from the federal domain, occurred all over the country throughout the nineteenth century. Large numbers of people were involved in such dealings, and a good measure of it was unavoidable under the circumstances of the times. Even the most idealistic settler risked much, including his life and that of his family, when he sought to create a farm out of frontier wilderness. But many of the speculators were no settlers at all. Many national and local leaders, from George Washington down to Sinclair Lewis' country doctor, bought and sold land for profit; and much of this still goes on. Many arguments have raged over the role of the land speculator in the national economy.

Did he perform a useful service, and if so, of what importance? The fact that many speculators made large fortunes does not automatically mean that they gained this money from someone else who lost in the process; at least in some cases, it has been argued, the speculator contributed to the more rapid settlement of large tracts in an orderly manner. Buying land from a dealer was often more efficient than the slow bureaucratic procedures of government agents. In other cases, of course, the speculator was more nearly a parasite. The balance is difficult to strike.

The land disposal process was often wasteful too. Speculation entails waste, to the extent that it diverts productive energies which could otherwise have been devoted to more productive endeavors (if such were available then and there). Many attempts at settlement involved waste because they were made in unsuitable locations or with insufficient preparation and experience. Settlement proceeded by trial and error, with plenty of the latter.

It has also been argued, more recently, that the nation might have been better off by moving more slowly and by establishing more intensive land use practices from the outset, which could have secured higher productivity at earlier dates. Intensive farming is usually more profitable than extensive practices, and a vast territory is a liability because of the huge overheads for transportation and other servies. The same argument is still raging in Brazil, where advocates of gradual expansion from the coast criticize the founding of Brazilia and the efforts of spreading new settlements in the wilderness as being too costly.

In regard to the United States, the argument is of course a moot one, for no one can redo past history. The economic losses of rapid settlement at that time largely fell on individuals—the unsuccessful settler and others who lost in the general atomistic struggle for survival. For our purpose we must characterize the land disposal process as it took place, for it was an essential

70

part of building a nation. The drive of the country and its people was not to be braked, and with all the mistakes made under way, the end product was magnificent. In little more than a century the United States had developed from a fringe along the Atlantic Coast to a continental nation, vastly larger in population as well as in area, with a highly productive economic system based, initially, on farms, forests, and mines. The wisdom of hindsight is not a fair basis for judgment, for each generation acts on what it has and what it believes. We need history to understand the present, not to pretend to be wiser than the founders of a nation.

CHAPTER 8

Farm Land Use and Farm Production

AGRICULTURAL LAND USE IN MODERN TIME

The first settlement often resulted in subsistence or semi-subsistence farms, producing a wide array of goods for the use of the farm family and the local community. As the Midwest and Far West were settled in an age of improving communications, farming became more specialized as it went westwards, and the process of specialization has continued since then. As of now, a number of "commodity belts" can be distinguished on the economic map of the United States.

Of the 1,150 million acres in farms and ranches in the 48 contiguous states, about 400 million are in cropland (including fallow cropland, crop failure, etc.). About 525 million acres are in pasture of varying degrees of improvement and productivity, and some 200 million acres are in forest. Of the cropland, more than half is used to raise feed crops—mainly feed grains, but also hay, silage, and other forage crops. Most of the acreage in the country is thus used for livestock production. This is because the high level of income permits a large consumption of meat. If incomes had been too low to permit a high meat consumption, or if people were largely vegetarian, then the same acreage could support several times as many people. This is true not only of the vast quantities of grain crops now used as stockfeed, but also of large acreages of land now used as pasture which might be used to grow crops; in such use, their yield would be low, but still the output in terms of food calories would be higher than it is now.

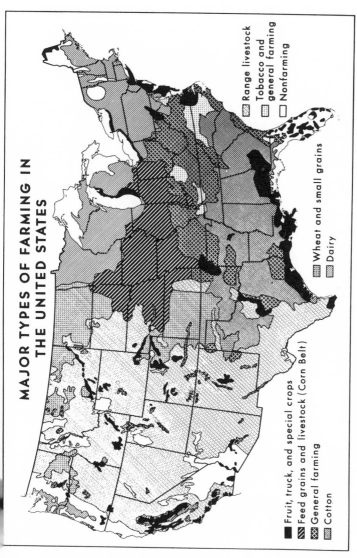

MAJOR TYPES OF FARMING IN THE UNITED STATES

Legend:
- Fruit, truck, and special crops
- Feed grains and livestock (Corn Belt)
- General farming
- Cotton
- Wheat and small grains
- Dairy
- Range livestock
- Tobacco and general farming
- Nonfarming

Fig. 11—Major Types of Farming in the United States

Slightly more than 50 million acres are used to produce food grains, chiefly wheat. The *Wheat Belt* is a vast north-south band around the 100th meridian, from Texas to North Dakota and Montana; a secondary wheat area lies in the Northwest, in the states of Washington, Oregon, and Idaho. Some wheat is also grown elsewhere, for instance in the Corn Belt, as an element of diversification in the cropping system. In times past, when the need for wheat was relatively greater, even larger acreages have been in such use. Even so, the United States produces twice as much wheat than is consumed within the country; the rest is exported in one way or another, despite obvious difficulties.

Cotton has remained one of the most important cash crops ever since the early nineteenth century. The *Cotton Belt* used to be almost identical with the "Deep South," but in recent decades it has both shrunk and shifted westward. Acreage has varied considerably, but in recent years it has not taken much more than 10 million acres. Cotton has declined considerably in the old plantation areas of the Southeast, where soil erosion has pointed to the need for forest planting on steep sites, and where other crops became more profitable in many cases. The lower Mississippi Valley has held its position as a major cotton area, but new ones have come up on irrigated land, in Texas and California and elsewhere in the West.

In the center of the country, from western Ohio to eastern Nebraska, the *Corn Belt* occupies much of the best farmland in the United States and in the world. Twelve states in this general area produce half of the farm output of the whole country. Although corn is the main crop, most of the output for final consumption is animal products, chiefly beef and pork. Corn as a cash crop is sold mainly to other farmers, through various intermediaries, for use as stockfeed. Cash corn farming is the dominant feature mainly in an area of central Illinois (the "black prairie") and in northwestern Iowa. Corn for human consumption is a very small part of all corn produced, in contrast to what obtains in Latin America or southeastern Europe.

As a cash crop, soybeans have become nearly as important as corn in many parts of the Corn Belt. Soybean meal is used mainly for stockfeed but is also used increasingly as an ingredient in many bakery products. Soybean oil is one of the important sources of fats for all kinds of uses. Large quantities of soybeans are exported.

To the north and east of the Corn Belt, cooler and not quite so fertile areas form the *Dairy Belt* in New England, the Lake States, and parts of the Middle Atlantic states. Another dairy belt is located along the northern Pacific Coast (in the states of Washington and Oregon). There are, of course, also areas with large dairy production near the large cities in all parts of the country. Milk consumption has been rather stationary over a long period of time, and, with rising milk yields, dairy farming could hardly be expected to expand; quite to the contrary, new strains of corn have made the Corn Belt expand, and the Dairy Belt shrink, especially in Minnesota.

The vast semiarid to arid areas in the West, in and around the Rocky Mountains, are clearly indicated mainly for pastoral husbandry, and this general area can therefore be designated as a *Ranching Belt*, with cattle as the principal line of production and sheep as a secondary one. These dry pastures would not respond to fertilization, their output of grass is rather constant in the long run if heavily fluctuating from year to year, and output in these areas is increasing mainly through the effect of new irrigation projects, many of them established with federal subsidies.

Other areas of specialized farming include the areas of *horticultural specialties* in the California Central Valley, along the Gulf Coast, and in Florida; and the *tobacco* areas in the Carolinas, Virginia, Tennessee, and Kentucky. Between the southeastern cotton and tobacco areas on the one hand, and the Corn and Dairy Belts on the other, a large east-westerly area, from Delaware and Virginia to southern Missouri, is usually described as the *General Farming* area, indicating a low degree of

75

specialization and an unusually high degree of production for consumption on the same farm. In these areas, as well as elsewhere in the Southeast, for instance, a variety of other crops makes specialization less evident; soybeans and peanuts are important, and in recent years many small subsistence farms have been converted into specialized broiler producers.

These areas of specialized farming are symptomatic of a high degree of economic specialization within the country; the exceptions, foremost the general-farming area, represent localized lags in economic development. These various farming situations also have important bearings upon the land tenure and farm organization, as we shall see below, and cannot but impinge upon the type of rural society that exists and can be expected to exist in the future.

TRENDS IN CROP YIELDS AND OUTPUT

American agriculture has changed during most of its history. The recent changes, say, since around 1920, are often referred to as "the agricultural revolution"; but, as often happens, the revolutionary change is really the accelerated fruition of changes under way for a long time.

As previously mentioned, colonial agriculture started with the most primitive manual methods and gradually acquired the full array of European technology as it existed at the time and as it continued to develop throughout the late eighteenth and early nineteenth century. Wooden ploughs were followed by iron ploughs only when the metal industries could produce hardware in adequate quantity. In America, the incentive toward technical innovation in agriculture was stronger than in the Old World in the nineteenth century, for the abundance of land and the scarcity of manpower created a situation we may term "pressure of resources upon people."

One hundred and sixty acres of land in the Midwest was a very generous allowance in the decades before the Civil War,

76

and even 80 acres gave a thrifty family a good living by the standards of the epoch. Forty to fifty acres was all that a farm family could place in crops with the tools in hand; the rest was used as pasture and as forest for fuel and fenceposts.

Expansion across the Midwest and the Great Plains placed a challenge to elementary technical inventiveness: how to fence cropland to protect it against grazing livestock and also to keep pigs within the land parcels on which they consumed the corn crop without the intervention of harvesting machines; and, even more, how to speed up plowing, planting, and harvesting so that farmers could command the full resource potential of their farms which appeared so large at that time. Some solution to the fencing problem was created in the humid Midwest through the "osage orange," a thorny shrub; but the real revolution in land use on the Great Plains depended on the coming of barbed wire.

Mowing machines had been attempted in Europe with moderate success, but in North America the need was so much greater, and it was in this country that the grain binder was made operational in the 1870's; the same breakthrough was made in Australia just a few years later. These and several other inventions made in the same decades were largely responsible for a rise in productivity in American agriculture that permitted the transition to urban-industrial society at a rapid pace, and without the need for a much denser farm population to fully cultivate all of the rich cropland potential of the country.

How dramatic were these developments is sometimes overlooked by a later generation which takes them for granted. At the start of the present century, productivity in United States agriculture was much higher than in most parts of the world. The end of spatial expansion was achieved during World War I. The rise of productivity continued most visibly after the middle of the 1930's and drew largely on "a storehouse of knowledge" which had already existed for some time. In the 1940's and 1950's, American agriculture saw its productivity rise at a record rate, even surpassing the contemporary trend in industry.

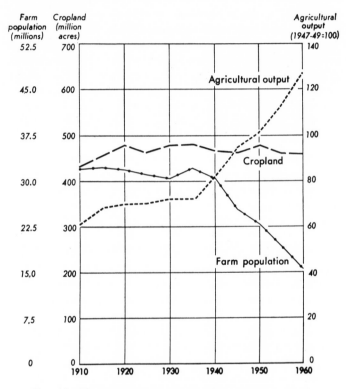

FIG. 12—TRENDS IN AGRICULTURAL OUTPUT, CROP LAND, AND FARM POPULATION SINCE 1910

The current agricultural revolution in the United States is revealed by this chart. From the same area of crop land, with half as many people on the farm, agricultural output more than doubled in fifty years. These changes are still under way, and further dramatic developments are probable over the next fifty years or less.

The rise in output, since 1920, has of course depended more than anything on increasing per-acre yields of important crops such as corn; in part it has depended on the placing of larger acreage in crops which yield more value per acre—including some essentially new crops such as the soybean; and to some extent, finally, the increase has come from new irrigation systems and other melioration projects.

The higher per-acre yield of several individual crops comes from a variety of technical innovations: improved varieties, more and cheaper fertilizers, better insect and disease control, greater ability to perform crop operations at the proper season, etc.

New inventions were made in many different ways, and their application was spread by a variety of channels, too. In an early phase of progress, typical of the mid-nineteenth century, simple improvements on the traditional tools were often made by village blacksmiths or by active farmers. Later, machine-building industries went ahead with developing new or improved machines; the grain binder is in this category. Since the late part of the nineteenth century, the colleges of agriculture, in the "land-grant" universities existing in all states, have increasingly been engaged in research and development of agricultural engineering, chemistry, biology, and economics. The Extension Service working out from these same colleges have carried the results of these and other research and development efforts to farmers and have thus—along with the salesmen working for farm supply industries—contributed to accelerating the progress and productivity of American agriculture.

The "agricultural revolution" is not over, but will continue for a long time. All of the gains in efficiency in ordinary field crops have not been made yet, and in regard to vegetables and fruits, intensive experimentation promises to set in motion new machines that will greatly improve productivity, perhaps also expand output; only a minor part of these innovations are as yet a reality. In animal husbandry, new techniques of feeding may yet revolutionize other lines of production as they already have in poultry production.

The rate of progress in recent decades is spectacular, yet it is understated in the actual production figures, for efforts are made to prevent production from rising even more. Surplus output is expensive to store and poses a threat to product prices. Only during the world wars and their aftermath has United States agriculture been producing to capacity. Rising technical efficiency expands that capacity, but agricultural policy looking to the welfare of farmers does its best to slow down the net result which takes the shape of added output.

There are many reasons why individual farmers adopt new technology and increase their output, even when the result for all farmers taken together is to lower prices to the point where incomes are no higher, and may be lower, under the new than under the old technology. The amount any one farmer can produce is so small, in comparison with total output, that he properly ignores the effect of his output on prices of the commodities he produces. Many farms—perhaps most of them— have some surplus labor; if some means can be found to employ it productively, income on that farm will be increased. Much of the new farm technology is output-increasing in effect. The farmer who adopts it increases his output, and the farmer who does not fails to increase his output, and each gets the same price on the market. It is therefore logical that farm output should be at a level where surpluses are chronic, when the ability to produce rises faster than the economic demand for the products.

In this way much of the progress in agriculture has seeped through to consumers, rather than staying in the hands of farmers. In real terms, the price of food and fiber raw material in the United States has fallen to half the level it had around 1930; in other words, the average consumer now sacrifices half as large a part of his income to pay for farm goods as he did three to four decades ago.

For farmers, this has the consequence of placing an increasing squeeze on their financial position. It becomes more and more difficult to own a full-sized farm, even through a lifetime of savings. Traditional concepts of land tenure are called in question by these recent tendencies in the farm economy.

CHAPTER 9

Farm Land Ownership and Tenure

The historical processes described in the previous chapters have produced the patterns of land ownership and land tenure which exist in the United States in modern time. About a third of the area of the country (including Alaska) is still federal domain; part of this area has never ceased to be federal property, while other areas have been acquired from private owners. Much of this land is unproductive or very low-productive. Other public bodies also own land, although to a far smaller extent than the federal government. Most of the high-productive land is private property.

Out of the nearly two thirds of the country that is in private ownership, about 80 percent is in farms. This is also about half of the total area of the country. This includes far more than the crop and pasture land we usually associate with farms. One third of all commercial forest in the country is in farms, and about one-seventh of the farm area is classified as commercial forest. In addition, relatively large acreages of low-grade grazing land and of noncommercial forest are found within farms. The number of farms reached its peak in the early part of the present century, with about six and a half million. Since the late 1930's, it has fallen at an accelerating rate, and is now around three million (see Table I).

The total area in farms increased not only during the years when farm numbers increased because the settled area was expanding, but also in recent decades; this is largely due to the inclusion into farms and ranches of grazing lands and forest areas previously not counted as parts of farms. Many ranches

82

which used to have "grazing permits" on federal land now have lease contracts on such land instead, which makes it part of land in farms. In addition, many ranchers still have "grazing permits," so that the total area used for farm production is even larger than the total area of all land in farms.

TABLE I

NUMBER OF FARMS, ALL LAND IN FARMS, AVERAGE FARM SIZE, AND PERCENTAGE OF ALL LAND THAT IS IN FARMS, 1850–1959

Year	Number of farms (thousands)	All land in farms (million acres)	Average size of farm (acres)	Percent of land area in farms
1850	1,449	294	203	15.6
1860	2,044	407	199	21.4
1870	2,660	408	153	21.4
1880	4,009	536	134	28.2
1890	4,565	623	137	32.7
1900	5,740	841	147	44.1
1910	6,366	881	139	38.8
1920	6,454	959	149	42.2
1930	6,295	990	157	43.6
1940	6,102	1,065	175	46.8
1950	5,388	1,163	216	51.1
1959	3,711	1,124	303	49.5

Source: U.S. Bureau of Census, *Census of Agriculture, 1959, General Report*, p. 369.

FARM LAND OWNERSHIP

The figures shown in the table are from the Census of Agriculture, and they show farms, i.e., operational units, rather than ownership units. In states and areas where most farms are owner-operated, the two concepts of operational units and ownership units are of course close to each other. Even in many areas where tenant farming prevails, ownership of tenant-operated land is widely scattered among numerous land owners, most of whom are persons of modest means. Various studies indicate that half or more of the owners of rented land are, or were, farmers; some are still active, more have retired and rent

83

their farms to younger men. Other owners include widows of farmers, business and professional men in small towns, and housewives. Some farm land is owned by relatively large-scale absentee owners, corporate or individual, but in total this area is relatively small. Despite the high incidence of tenancy in some areas, ownership of farm land is widely distributed.

Large-scale ownership of farm land occurs as a minor feature in many parts of the country, but it is of major importance in the same areas where large operational units exist to greater extent. The areas concerned are, principally, the cotton plantation areas of the South; part of the ranching areas in the Rocky Mountains; and the California Central Valley with its high-intensive speciality crop cultivation. These are also much the same areas in which large-scale property and large-scale farming became established at some early date. But not all of the originally existing large-scale land ownership survived the economic pressures of the country's expansionist decades.

Thus, for instance, much more large-scale property had once existed in what is now the Corn Belt. In part, these large landholdings were held for speculation; they were thus intended to be sold to whoever proved capable of buying them to farm. In other cases, such early large landholdings were intended as large ranching or farming units, but many such units fell apart for one reason or another. For instance, in central Illinois, on the Black Prairie, there were once "cattle kingdoms," at the time when Chicago was an incipient small town and the market prospects for large grain crops had not yet materialized. The dissolution of such large units was not simply due to economic failure on the part of their owners. In part it reflected the necessity to switch from ranching to crop farming, and the difficulty to grow corn with a large hired labor force in a country where wages were relatively high. But more than anything it was due to the pressures from the open frontier and the generous land market. Despite all the fraud and speculation, which we have touched upon above, laws such as the Pre-emption Act and the

84

Homestead Act became safety valves against any attempt on the part of speculators to gain any kind of complete control of the land market. The railroad grants and the various land grants to states also provided additional outlets for a market supply of cheap land which was too large to permit land prices to rise very high. This made it in most cases more profitable for large landowners to sell to prospective farm owners rather than to try their hand at large-scale farming. In this way the land laws of the United States did reach their central purpose, despite all the shortcomings both in their co-ordination and in their implementation. The intermediate solution of the large landowner's problem, to rent land to tenant farms, was less unsafe than that of large-scale operation, and was also used somewhat more often. A few large properties in the Corn Belt survived from the age of speculation in this manner.

The southern plantations are, of course, a direct continuation of the plantation system at the time of slavery economy, which was a means of arresting the pressure from high wages and cheap land, which would otherwise have made the large land-holdings crumble. The semibondage, in which many of the freed slaves remained in the aftermath of the Civil War, gave the plantations a chance to survive, but they too had to use tenancy contracts of a peculiar type ("cropper contracts"), as we shall see below. Many of the large ranches in the Far West also had to disappear, among other things because the ranchers had trespassed on federal land and so were ousted from possession of some of this land. Others survive to this day, for reasons too complex to go into here. The large holdings in California, finally, were formed and could survive, in part because this remote area never attracted *farm settlers* on anything like the scale of the Midwest and the Great Plains. California grew from its coastal cities; mining was important at an early date, and an industrial economy grew up here earlier than in many areas located nearer to the center of the continent. Land hunger was therefore not the same as elsewhere. Even so, it is clear that the existence of large landholdings and large farms in the California Central Valley is due as much to historical factors as to any advantage of such a system in the present situation.

FARM NUMBERS AND SIZE

Returning to Table I, we can see how the settlement of the Midwest and Far West was accompanied by a decline in the average size of farm. In part, this reflects the dissolution of many of the early large holdings; in part, it is due to the transition of southern plantations from central operation to the cropper system, as we shall describe below. At the same time, of course, westward expansion to drier areas led to the establishment of many farms and ranches of larger acreage than those in the more humid and more early settled parts of the Midwest. All told, this movement of farm size reflected a parallel movement of land ownership, which became more and more widespread.

The beginning decline in farm numbers in the 1920's was temporarily interrupted during the crisis of the early 1930's; the 1935 census (not quoted in the table) had an even higher farm number than any preceding census. This was short-lived, however, and since the late 1930's the number of farms has declined more and more rapidly. This decline in farm numbers, and the consequent rise in average farm size, in part reflects a renewed tendency toward consolidation of southern plantations; most of the cropper holdings have been discontinued and their land integrated with the central operation of the plantation. The rise in farm size is general, however, all over the country, as far as size in acres is concerned. But there has not been any corresponding increase in farm size measured by its use of manpower. Most farms are still "family-scale" operations, and most of the farm production in the country (two thirds or more) comes from family-scale farms. By family-scale farms is meant those farms where the farmer and his family members do most of the work. The proportion against "large-scale" farms (those where hired laborers do most of the work) has hardly changed in recent time, for with machinery, the area that can be farmed by a family is larger than before. The share of hired labor in the total labor requirement of American farms has also not changed much, and most of the work on farms is still done by the farmers themselves with help of their families.

There are differences in this respect too, by areas and by type of farms. The old cotton plantations are now often consolidated anew, as centrally operated large farms. The decline in number of croppers has then been accompanied by a smaller but significant increase in the use of hired labor on these plantations. This then partially offsets the decline in the use of hired labor elsewhere, as in the Corn Belt, the dairy areas, and the Wheat Belt. The California large farms are to a great extent specialized in horticultural and other labor intensive production requiring much hired labor which also, by the nature of the situation, has to be cheap labor. Rising labor cost in recent years are met with more and more mechanization also of vegetable production. Many family farmers also use low-paid migrant farm workers for specialty crops such as fruits and vegetables. Large-scale ranchers, by contrast, have found that not only do they have to pay hired hands quite good wages, but sometimes they also find it advantageous to offer profit sharing to herdsmen with a large measure of independent responsibility.

Large-scale economy is, however, invading the family-scale farm system from other angles than through outright farm enlargement. For instance, most of the new poultry broiler farms in Delaware-Maryland, Georgia, and elsewhere, are technically independent, family-scale operations, and such operations produce most of the poultry meat in the country. But economically the operators of such farms are often little more than the hired agents of large-scale "integrators" who hold the keys to supply of the highly perfected chicken feed as well as to the timely and large-scale selling of the output. A reason why the integrators do not consolidate the operations and use outright hired labor is that the family-farm system spreads the risk, making each unsuccessful operator pay for his own mistakes. In a somewhat different way, many of the fruit farms in Florida are owned by small-scale investors who are only nominally farm operators, while all the cultivation and spraying is done by service companies, and the fruit is bought on the trees by the fruit corporations who use their own crews for the harvesting.

The total share of family-scale farming in the country's agriculture is thus somewhat smaller than conventional figures would indicate. The core of American farming—in corn and wheat growing, dairying, hog raising and cattle fattening—is still essentially family-scale industry and has as yet not been penetrated by any large-scale financial interests, even though there is much discussion about how far "vertical integration" will take the traditionally free and atomistic farming community.

It is interesting to see how far this family-farm system still bears the imprint of the original land division as it was carried out through the measurement and disposal of the federal domain. In the Midwest, most new farms were once of either 80 or 160 acres, or some area approximating one of these sizes. Even though farms are now, on the whole, much larger, the sizes 80 acres and 160 acres still occur with considerably higher frequency than would follow from a random walk of events on a land market (sale and rental) without any institutional inhibitions. Another feature is the more narrow spread of farm sizes around the mean in the public-domain areas that became settled under the pre-emption and homestead laws. This spread around the mean is a kind of index of socio-economic disparity in the community. This spread is unusually narrow in the Midwest, indicating an unusually high degree of "distributive equity" in the distribution of property in the community. The spread is much wider in the plantation areas of the South, indicating a much lower degree of distributive equity. These conditions in regard to the spread of farm sizes around the mean have been surprisingly constant over time; as far back as we can follow them, they have been very nearly the same as now in the various parts of the country, with very nearly the same differences, say, in 1880, 1935, and 1959. This points up the significance of the land system that is laid down in a formative phase of a nation; despite all the subsequent economic and political events, the men who favored the homestead and the plantation, respectively, left the imprint of their intentions to decide the lives of many coming generations.

The decline in farm numbers has been accompanied by a proportionate decline in the agricultural population. As already pointed out, the relative role of hired labor has not increased; but it has become somewhat differently distributed. The socioeconomic change represented by the decline in farms is still going on, and the outlook to the future should be commented upon briefly. The trend of the past, and some projections toward the future, are shown in Figure 13.

The decline in farm numbers depends, of course, foremost on the continued industrialization of the country. From the beginning until the Civil War and even thereafter, the United States was mainly an agricultural country. With rapid growth in population, a movement of people from the dominant farm sector to the much smaller urban sector was practically difficult and hardly desirable as long as farming expanded over virgin land. In a later phase, when the farmers began to be a minority, and all the land was occupied, the number of farms and farmers ceased to increase, and the population increment could go to other occupations. As late as in 1910, one third of all Americans were farmers; in 1930, one fourth. In such a situation, obviously, a rapid reduction in the number of farmers would have created embarrassing problems on the urban labor market.

The peak numbers of farms were reached around 1935, when there were about 6.5 million farms in the United States. Many of these were quite small, not only in area but also in the volume of their production. A tract of three acres or more, producing $250 or more worth of agricultural products, was classed as a farm. More than a fourth were self-sufficient farms—i.e., more of their total production was consumed on these farms than was sold from them; or they were part-time farms, enterprises on which the operator spent only part of his time, while working for wages (in agriculture or elsewhere) the rest of his active

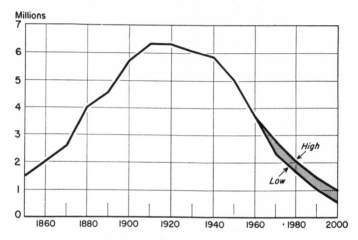

FIG. 13—NUMBER OF FARMS IN THE UNITED STATES, 1850–1960, AND PROJECTIONS TO 2000

As western settlement moved swiftly forward, the number of farms in the United States more than trebled from 1850 to 1910. Following thirty years of roughly constant numbers, substantial reductions took place, bringing us today back to fewer farms than in 1880. Major further reductions in farm numbers seem inevitable, and by 2000 we probably shall have many fewer farms than in 1850.

time. Nearly another one-fourth of all the farms produced less than $2,500 worth of total output, measured in terms of today's prices, which was supposed to give the family their sole or main source of income. Although these small farms had relatively low cash operating costs at that time, they obviously could not have large net incomes. This state of affairs was wearily tolerated as

90

long as the urban incomes were also much lower than now and urban unemployment more threatening.

The major changes in farm numbers which have taken place since 1935 are closely linked with a number of concurrent changes, in the economy in general as well as in the agricultural economy. Despite the rapid rate of decline, we can still note that the decline has been even more rapid in the number of young farmers. The older men often could not enter into another occupation and thus found themselves trapped in farming as a low-income situation. The young were usually better educated than the older people and hence more employable in alternative occupations. Wartime experience in the armed forces also had taught many of them mechanical skills which could be used in other occupations. At the same time, as the agricultural population became a smaller and smaller fraction of the total, the absorption of those who wanted to leave farming into other occupations became less and less of a problem. Rising urban incomes raised the income expectations of the young people on farms too. As the price of farm labor goes up, the economic advantage of replacing labor with capital is increasing. The now very large industrial economy is able to produce heavy farm equipment in large quantities, as it was not able to do several decades earlier. Equally important, these factory-produced means of farm production are offered at falling relative prices, at the same time as the relative price of labor is going up as it should in an economy with rising incomes. These concurrent factors produced the income squeeze on farmers which resulted in the precipitous decline in farm numbers.

The fall in farm numbers is naturally accompanied by a corresponding rise in average farm size, as long as size is measured in acres. When farm size is measured by some economic criterion, the picture is partly different. The United States Census of Agriculture uses a system of economic classification by size of total farm marketings (gross income from sales). The greatest reduction has been among the farms of less than $2,500 gross

91

income, in terms of today's prices; they declined from 3.5 million in 1935 to 1.5 million in 195, and are still declining rapidly. Farms of the next larger size-class, those with $2,500 to $5,000 gross income, have also declined in numbers during the same period, but not so drastically. Larger farms have increased in number—the largest sizes the most, comparatively. These changes in farm numbers according to "economic class"

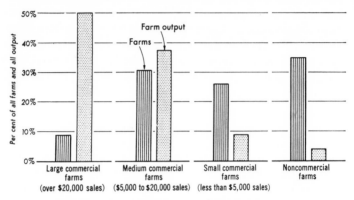

FIG. 14—FARM OUTPUT BY SIZE OF FARM, 1959

There is enormous variation in the productivity of farms in the United States. At one extreme are the noncommercial farms, a third of the total number but with less than 5 percent of total output; at the other extreme, less than 10 percent of the largest farms produce just half of the whole agricultural output. The small commercial farms seem to have no real economic future; their output is so low that no price level can make them profitable.

are partly due to many smaller ones actually ceasing to operate and to the establishment of many larger ones through consolidation of land from smaller farms; to some extent, however, the same farmer with the same basic farm unit has found ways of increasing his farm output to such an extent that his farm has become reclassified in a higher economic size-class. At the same time, farm operating expenses as a proportion of gross farm income have risen, so that the same gross farm income today may not represent as large a net income as it did twenty years or more ago (this on the basis of the same prices in each period). In this way, the "economic classification" of farms by size of their gross sales tends to exaggerate the rise in farm size.

The best indications are that future changes in farm numbers and farm size will be a continuation of these trends, at least for the next two decades and maybe longer. Young men will leave farming, either because the prospect of taking over a small farm is not attractive enough, or because there is no farm holding or other farm job available to them. Older men will withdraw only as death and retirement normally take them out. The result will be fewer farmers than at present, and the average age of the group will continue to go up yet for some time.

FARM TENURE CHANGES

As pointed out above, the original settlement in each area left as a result a farm structure where most farms were operated by their owners. In most of the country, this meant preponderantly family farms, worked by their owners and their families with little if any hired help. Some amount of tenancy existed, but not on any large scale. In the southeastern states, the plantation areas, there were also many small family farms, but economically the scene was dominated by the plantation, worked with numerous slaves; usually the plantation was managed by its owner, too.

After the Civil War, tenancy began to gain importance. The first sign came in the old plantation areas, where the landowners found it expedient to use the freed slaves under a type of rental contract, known as the "cropper" system. The landlord supplied the land, work stock, tools, seed, and other necessities; the "cropper" usually supplied only his labor, undertook the production within relatively narrow limits set by the instructions given by the landlord, and got a certain fraction of

93

the output as his income. The advantage to the landlord was that the cropper shared in the risk and thus had some, if not very strong, incentive to work for a satisfactory crop. Gradually, as the existence of cotton croppers came to sight in the Census of Agriculture, the Old South became the first area where tenant farming was recognized as important. There has been some difference of opinion as to the character of this system: is the cropper really an operator or a hired worker? On some occasions, the census has supplied tabulations also of the landlords as managerial units: the "multiple-unit operation," which sheds some light on the operation of plantations through croppers.

In other parts of the country, tenancy was slower to gain momentum. Yet it came as a shock to many who regarded the owner-farmer as an essential part of the American heritage when the early censuses showed not only that tenancy was more widespread than usually assumed, but also that it was on the increase.

Starting from certain areas of concentration in the Midwest, tenancy gradually spread and became important throughout the Midwest and on the Great Plains. From the time when most of the good farm land was already occupied, land prices (which had been low until then) rose sharply through several decades, thus making it more and more difficult to buy a farm out of savings from wage work or tenant farming. A peak in land prices was reached in 1910; with a short inflationary interruption around 1920, land prices thereafter fell gradually and reached their low point in the mid-1930's, toward the end of the Great Depression. The entire period of falling land prices was on the whole one of depressed conditions for agriculture, reflected among other things in very slow rises in productivity. Falling land prices were a threat to all those who had a mortgage loan on their farms, and many mortgages were foreclosed, especially during the Great Depression of the early 1930's. In 1935, 41 percent of all farms were operated by tenants. Tenant

94

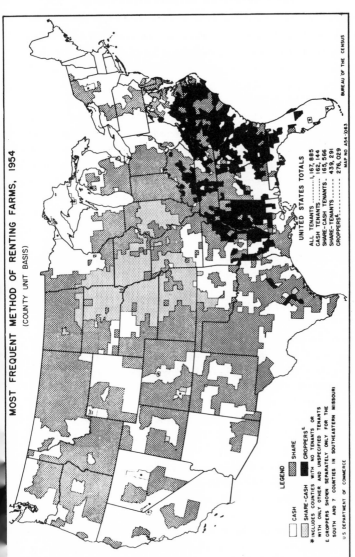

MOST FREQUENT METHOD OF RENTING FARMS, 1954

(COUNTY UNIT BASIS)

LEGEND

CASH

SHARE-CASH

SHARE

CROPPERS*ᴸ

* INCLUDES COUNTIES WITH NO TENANTS OR
WITH ONLY OTHER AND UNSPECIFIED TENANTS

ᴸ CROPPERS SHOWN SEPARATELY ONLY FOR THE
SOUTH AND 7 COUNTIES IN SOUTHEASTERN MISSOURI

U.S. DEPARTMENT OF COMMERCE

UNITED STATES TOTALS

ALL TENANTS	1,167,885
CASH TENANTS	162,144
SHARE-CASH TENANTS	165,566
SHARE-TENANTS	439,291
CROPPERSᴸ	276,029

BUREAU OF THE CENSUS

MAP NO A54-1063

Fig. 15—Counties in which at least Half of the
Farms Were Operated by Tenants
1880, 1900, 1920, 1930, 1940, 1950, and 1954

farms were smaller than the average of all farms when the size criterion is total area, but they were larger in cropland area—together they accounted for one third of the cropland. Much of this cropland was in the best farming areas of the country, and tenant farms thus accounted for an even larger share of all the productive resources. In addition, of course, many farmers were heavily in debt, so that in net terms, farm operators owned much less than half of all the value of farm land. A partial offset is in the fact that many tenant farmers, and many contract-buyers too, are the sons and heirs of their landlords and contract-sellers, respectively. In fact, a large part of the landlords are farmers or former farmers, and resource control is therefore in the hands of the farmer population to a greater extent than the above summary would indicate. The total balance is difficult to evaluate.

From the late 1930's, the trend of change in farm tenure was reversed. Farm price supports were accompanied by a new tendency toward higher productivity in agriculture, and, in the aftermath of the depression, farm land was still relatively cheap and thus easier to acquire for those who had savings and a good credit standing. Inflation reduced the real value of old mortgage loans and made them easier to repay. The immediate postwar years provided very good incomes to American farmers. The old ideal of owner-farmer with moderate mortgage debt seemed revived.

This new trend petered out in the course of the 1950's. At least in some parts of the country, tenancy is again on the increase, if at a moderate pace. Usually this takes the form of mixed tenure—part ownership, part tenancy, as a means of building up larger operations. Mortgage debt is still of moderate proportions, even though rising slowly. Another method of financing land purchase has gained importance: the installment land contract, which had some importance during the nineteenth century but was almost unknown a few decades ago. Under this form of financing, the debt ceiling is much higher and the risk incurred by the buyer, that he lose some of his money if he defaults, is much greater. Many land contracts are family transactions, however, and in these cases the consequence of default is different from the case of unrelated buyer and seller.

At the same time as farm prosperity of the 1940's and early 1950's reduced tenancy in most parts of the country, the cropper system of the South has declined for partly different reasons. Increasingly, the owners of plantations have switched back to the use of hired labor, and most of the cropper contracts have been discontinued. This reflects above all heavy mechanization of the cultivation of cotton and other crops, which sharply reduced the need for labor. The tenure change looks like one away from tenancy toward operation by the owner; but the gain in owner-operatorship goes to the landlords who consolidate the operation of their holdings. Socially this is quite different from the decline in tenancy in other areas. The economics of it also is somewhat different, because many croppers found themselves without a job in the new situation and, knowing no other trade or craft, they went to the cities to swell the ranks of the frequently unemployed, unskilled drudgery workers.

Even now, it is difficult to say who owns most of the resources of American agriculture. Adding together the land under lease, the mortgage and land contract debt, and all the special financing—e.g., by integrators for specialized poultry production, citrus groves, etc.—and add to this the sector of large-scale farms (above all in the cotton areas, the California specialty areas, and part of the ranches), then it becomes clear that family-scale operating farmers own only a minor part of the productive resources of agriculture. They still control the larger part of the production, but only because so much of their resources are held under lease or credit financed.

The statistics on ownership and tenancy tell only part of the story, however. Especially when comparison is made with other countries, differences in custom with regard to family property and inheritance must be kept in mind. In the United States a formal contract is often concluded between close relatives; many American tenant farmers rent their farms from their aged parents. In some other countries, the old farmer remains formally in control all his life, and the son who actually does the farming is then counted as a family member, not as a "non-landowning farmer." In this way, the share of farm resources that belong to farmer families is actually larger than the statistics would indicate.

Something similar is true of real-estate debt, especially in the form of installment credit ("land contract"), which is often used as a means of gradually transferring property to the younger generation of farmers.

Some part of the rationale for the occurrence of tenancy can be learned from the tenure maps as shown in Figure 15. Tenancy is dominant mainly in three of the specialized farming zones: the Corn Belt, the Wheat Belt, and the Cotton Belt. It is less significant in the Dairy Belt and not very important in the ranching areas. The areas of fruit and vegetable production also do not have much tenancy, even though some of the forms of "owner-operation" are peculiar. The poultry producers, as a rule, are also mostly owner-operators in the legal sense, even though their economic independence is nominal.

All this adds up to a distinct pattern. Tenant farming is most important in areas specialized in field crops for cash disposal. This is where risk is short-term and lease arrangements can be renewed from year to year without too much danger of impairing the resources. Tenancy is much less important in areas of specialized animal husbandry, which requires a longer planning horizon and runs more risk of destroying productive assets through frequent and short-term interruptions. The point is much less valid on poultry farms, but here too, the risk of loss through bad management is such that the integrators rather let the farmers carry it. Also tree crops require long-term planning, and stable tenure arrangements are more important there than in field crops. Vegetables are a less clear case, and there is a good deal of tenant farming with delivery contracts to food chains who sometimes also are landlords; the role of large-scale operation in vegetable production, e.g., in California, depends in part on historical reasons (how the federal domain was disposed of in those parts), in part also on the need for stable delivery contracts, to large-scale buyers, of the perishable output.

The general conclusion suggested above is borne out by a detailed study of the tenure map and its changes. For example, within the Corn Belt, tenancy is most important in two areas: east-central Illinois and northwestern Iowa. It also came into being there first, and as tenancy shrank generally, it tended to hold on most in precisely those areas. These are the areas in which cash-grain farming dominates over combined crop and livestock farming, which is more in evidence in other parts of the Corn Belt. These are also the areas in which land values are highest, and a landlord's income most dependable. Thus they are also the areas in which a prospective farm buyer would have the most difficulty in paying for a farm out of his savings as a tenant or laborer.

The terms of lease contracts are regulated by state law, not by federal law, and therefore it is not possible to summarize briefly what restrictions there are of what may go into a contract. On the whole the contracting parties have a wide range of freedom to contract as they may agree, and actual terms are decided more by custom than by law. Most leases are contracted for a short term at a time—one year is the most common lease period. Leases are often in written form, but many are unwritten, and local custom then is important as evidence of what the lease entailed. In most cases, the lease is automatically prolonged for the following year, unless notice to terminate is served at least four months before the expiration of the current contract. In practice, numerous tenants stay on the same farms for decades, some of them throughout a lifetime. Others may shift from year to year. Stability of tenure depends in practice

99

more on the availability of good tenant farmers than on the terms of the contract. Most landlords in the United States are persons of modest means who give on lease a single farm or a few farms, and they are often as anxious to keep a good tenant as the latter is to stay on the same farm.

These conditions too vary according to the area, its type of farming, and its prevalent type of lease. Most leases in the United States imply a share of the farm's output as rent or as a large part of the rent. Cash leases are thus a minor feature in the country as a whole and in most of its parts; they are somewhat more numerous than other leases in parts of the northeast Dairy Belt and in the California Central Valley—both areas of low incidence of tenancy. Crop-share lease with some cash rent is the dominant lease form in the cash-grain areas of Illinois and Iowa. Crop-share leases without any cash rent are common in the South (the same areas where "cropper" contracts are important), and to a lesser extent in the Corn Belt and the Great Plains. Livestock-share leases, which are really a kind of partnership between landlord and tenant, are important in the Corn Belt, mainly outside the cash-grain areas. The share paid under share leases is in most cases one half, but other proportions occur to a varying extent, especially in the South. Whenever there is a tendency for a change in the share proportions, this is taken as a symptom of a change in the asset value of land and a converse change in the value of operator labor associated with a given amount of land.

The variety of lease types and of share proportions point to the market function of leasing. Lease terms express the relative price of the factors of production. They do so with much imperfection, but their role is an indispensable regulator of factor markets.

In times past, the presence of a mixed tenure system (both operator-ownership and leasing being important in many areas) has been interpreted as a system of open opportunites for advancement of young farm people. This advancement was often thought of as an "agricultural ladder." A young man might start out as a hired hand, then advance to tenant farmer, later accumulate enough savings to buy a farm of his own, and perhaps finally be sufficiently well off to own some extra land which he leases ("farmer-landlord"), and finally retire to live on his savings and on the rent from his land. Thus there was a "ladder" of four or five "rungs" on which the industrious and the thrifty could advance economically and socially.

The functioning of such a ladder depends on several things, among which the concentration of property, the general availability of economic opportunity, and also, lately, the proportion between labor earnings and the volume of savings necessary to own or even to rent a farm. Already from the start, the ladder concept was rather unreal to the Negro croppers of the southern plantation areas. Elsewhere too, climbing the ladder might be more or less difficult owing to conditions as they existed in the area. Throughout the period up until World War I the ladder concept was working usefully in many parts of the country, and it contributed to the degree of social mobility and the lack of sharp class distinctions which characterized life in most of the United States but perhaps most of all in the Midwest. Social mobility is now largely (although far from perfectly) secured by other economic forces, but the classical ladder concept has become less and less operational as the capital requirements rose. To own a farm through most of his life, a farmer now should have inherited some of its value; to assemble it all through savings from his labor and management earnings is increasingly difficult. Some still do it in part on earnings from off-farm labor, but this too becomes more and more difficult as the capital requirements in farming go up.

This economic rationale of tenancy versus owner-operator arrangements is aided, in the modern situation, by another consideration. Size of operation is more important, under modern, capital-intensive conditions, than full ownership of resources. With the high level of capitalization, it is important for the

101

farmer to be as fully employed as he can. A young man with modest resources, who goes into farming, can secure a higher income by renting a large farm than by buying a small one. In the former case he can use his own capital to equip himself with machines and livestock, while as a small-scale owner he would, in fact, have less resources at his disposal. These realities find their expression, at present, in the large and increasing importance of the part-owner, part-tenant farms. On the average, they are the largest and the most prosperous. The reason why this form dominates and not the all-rented farm (which is on the decline, at the same time as the area under lease may increase) is in part that many farmers have inherited a farm which is now too small to farm alone, and in part that the successful operator, in his older days, uses his savings to buy land, which is the kind of investment he knows best and therefore trusts the most.

The increasing role of part-owner, part-tenant farms is one of the symptoms of a pressure toward changes in the tenure system. Others are visible in the search for new tenure arrangements and new modes of transfer of farm property to the next generation. We referred in the above to lease contracts and installment purchase contracts within the family; the latter also aims at reducing taxes on inheritance. There are many "father-son agreements" which aim at gradually transferring control to the younger generation. Recently a number of cases have come up where a family's farm property is incorporated as a business firm, which in some ways should render estate settlements easier while securing the intact continuation of the family farm. Professional farm managers often serve as a useful link between land owner and farm operator. Finally, many banks have begun to act as intermediaries between landlords and tenants, especially when the landlords are not farmers themselves; and the possibility is discussed of having such bank services transformed into "land trusts" which could achieve the dual goal of stability of tenure for the farm operator and ease of transfer of real

102

property between non-farm landowners. These incipient tendencies may or may not be pointers to future changes in the tenure system; in any event they are symptomatic of the need for changes when American farming has become one of the most highly capitalized industries of the modern world.

All of this does not mean that the old ideal of the owner-operating farmer was a mistake at the time when the ideal was formed. Jefferson and his followers lived at a time when farming consisted of land and labor, with very little capital. They had no reason to anticipate the problems of the late twentieth century in a highly industrialized society which has taken several generations to build up. The independence of pioneer farmers was a potent force in the expansion of the country and in the building of its institutions. The fact that it is now yielding to the increasing interdependence of production factors and social groups carries no denial of the merits of the past, nor does it automatically supply any clear-cut answer to the problem of the tenure forms which will best serve production and social life in the future.

CHAPTER 10

Forest Land Ownership and Management

Forests once covered half of the area of the 48 contiguous states of the United States. Most of the areas east of the Mississippi River were covered with forest, as were also large parts of the states immediately to the west of the same stream, and large areas in the Rocky Mountains and along the Pacific Coast.

To the early settlers, the forests seemed inexhaustible, and for a long time this was virtually true. Yet, in those days the forest, apart from being an obstacle to cultivation, had to serve as the main source of fuel as well as timber. With coal, oil, and gas, the fuel value of forests faded out, and, at the beginning of the present century, forests were valuable mainly as a source of building materials. Today the wood of the trees can be used in many new ways, among other things as raw material for the chemical industries. Forests are also now valued as an environment for recreation. The value of forest for watershed protection (flood control and erosion control) has also been recognized.

The early colonists had forests in such abundance that they wanted to get rid of them as much as possible. This attitude remained long after the supply of mature timber had dwindled and while new growth was often slow. Today a new attitude is at work. The much reduced forest areas are managed with a view to maintain sustained production. Within the last two decades or so, for the first time since generations, growth and removal (cut plus losses from fire, disease, and insects) are again in balance.

The ownership of forest land falls into five major categories. First there are the forests owned by the federal government; they cover less than one-fifth of the forested area but they contain more than two-fifths of the volume of standing timber. Second are the forests owned by public bodies other than the federal government (states, counties, and other local government). They are much smaller, with about 5 percent of the area and a slightly smaller proportion of the standing timber. Third, the forest industries own only slightly less area than the federal government, but these lands contain substantially less standing timber. Fourth are the farm forests, the largest among the ownership classes, with about a third of the total area but about half that percentage of the standing timber. Last there are private forests not owned by timber industries or in farms, the inevitable "other" classification. They are the next largest in area, after the farm forests, and more than twice as large as the forest industry holdings, but they have a relatively low volume of timber.

In general, the federal forests are well managed, as we will show below in Chapter 12. There are some deficiencies in the budget-appropriation processes, however. The other publicly owned forests are similarly managed, but not quite so well on the whole.

There are several problems about making forestry profitable on a sustained basis. Slow turnover and lack of liquidity makes many forest owners remove the trees as soon as they are at all marketable, which is of course poor forestry. This difficulty of small and medium-scale forestry is the main rationale for the prominent part played by the public powers as forest owners. With a longer tradition of sustained-yield forest management, there would be no reason why private forestry could not do as well, but it has to be on a large scale.

105

LARGER PRIVATE FORESTS

An economic unit for forestry operation has to be many times larger than a farm unit. On the average, forest land in the United States is about one-sixth as productive as cropland in farms. This average includes a wide variation (as does the cropland). A forestry enterprise, to sell sawlogs and pulpwood,

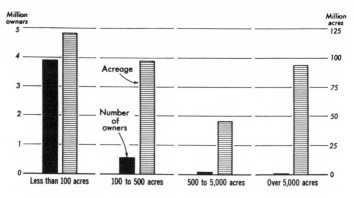

FIG. 16—FOREST AREA, BY SIZE OF HOLDING

The distribution of forest land among owners of various sizes is even more extreme than is the distribution of farm output among farms of different sizes. A minuscule percentage of the largest forests contain a fourth of the whole acreage, but 4 million of the smallest forests contain less than half of the whole area. The latter have little prospect of profitable return because of their small size.

with a minimum efficient harvesting crew on a year-round basis, should have from 10,000 to 20,000 acres in order to operate on a sustained-yield basis. This is perhaps the minimum size for a full-time operation; owners with less land can of course run part-time forestry enterprises with other employment during part of the year. The exact amount of minimum area varies with timber type and the kind of processing the wood is intended for. Many sawmills operate without owning any land, by buying timber wherever they can get it. There may be substantial economies to scale if timber volumes are large enough to provide a good annual harvest near the processing plant. Since World War II there has been a clear trend toward merging already relatively large wood-manufacturing firms into much larger ones. An area of a quarter million to a million acres is not exceptionally large for a large modern forest products manufacturing plant.

In 1953 there were about 300 private forest owners with 50,000 or more acres of forest land each. Most of these were forest industry firms, with processing plants of their own and forestry as their main interest. But some belonged to the "other" category mentioned above. These owners mainly sold timber to the larger processors. On the whole, these forests are as well managed as the federally owned forests. There were nearly 2,500 private forests of 5,000 to 50,000 acres in size, averaging about 14,000 acres each. As discussed above, these are just about minimum efficiency units for timber harvest but not for timber processing. These forests are, on the average, fairly well managed but not as well as the larger ones.

The larger private forests are scattered throughout the forested parts of the country. They are especially common in the Pacific region, where forestry operations are often relatively large; some are found in the South, especially such owned by companies making pulp and paper; and a few are found elsewhere. Some large forest owners operate in more than one region. In general the forests included in these larger holdings are naturally productive forests, and their present productivity is relatively high. With considerable variation both ways they offer, on the whole, a reasonable prospect for profitable forestry operation. Part of their area is poorly stocked, sometimes with unsuitable species; part needs replanting, and there are other deficiencies. But on the whole the prospect for maintaining these forests is good.

These larger forest owners have in general shown considerable

107

sensitivity to the public's demand for recreational use of their forests. Most owners permit hunting and fishing on their land, and many maintain campgrounds and other facilities, sometimes available free and sometimes against payment of a fee. In

Size of forest tract (acres)	Total acreage in this size class (millions of acres)	Economic prospects for good forestry (based on size alone)
Over 50,000	58	Good to excellent
5,000 to 50,000	35	Good
500 to 5,000	46	Fair to good; most such units are below optimum size to form an economic forest unit by themselves; most require some specialized management in addition to the owners; but some economic incentives to good forestry do exist on the larger tracts of better site quality.
100 to 500	98	Fair; such forests are often sidelines to some other economic activity; larger farm forests, if well stocked, may offer a fair prospect; poorer and smaller farm forests offer very little economic incentive; among "other" forests, the better ones offer some prospects if under some form of group or supervised management
Under 100	121	Poor to nonexistent, except in case of farm forests integrated with agricultural enterprise, or unless combined with other ownerships for management purposes.

FIG. 17—ECONOMIC POSSIBILITIES OF PRIVATE FORESTS

order to maintain good public relations, many larger forest owners hesitate to impose a use charge, even though the visiting public may increase their costs of maintenance.

SMALL PRIVATE FORESTS

The "small" privately owned forests in the United States are very numerous and very small on the average. Again we must remember that "small" as well as "large" means much larger areas in forestry than in farming. There are about 46,000 privately owned forests of 500 to 5,000 acres. These holdings contain about 10 percent of all commercial forest in the country. Their net productivity rating is very much lower than that of the forest industry holdings or the federal forests. About half of these forests are part of farms, most of the rest belong to various other categories of owners. If operated alone, these units would be far from being economic units. In combination with some other activity, some of them produce significant income.

Forests of 100 to 500 acres are more than ten times as numerous as the former group, and they contain twice as much land. Their net productivity ratings are even lower. There are nearly four million forest holdings below 100 acres, with still lower productivity ratings than any of the other categories. Their total area is considerable, however.

Many of these small privately owned forest holdings had inherently low productivity even when covered with virgin timber. The farm forest is often the land that is left over after all suitable land has been cleared for plowing or pasturing. Because of poor soil, steep slopes, unsuitable climate, or for other reasons, the rate of tree growth on such land has often been low all the time. Most of these forests have been cut, usually several times, generally in an exploitive manner. Some of these forests could be rehabilitated and made more productive. The measures needed (replanting, "weeding," sometimes drainage, etc.) carry high initial costs and will produce income only many years later. The large forest owner can absorb such costs as part of the normal replenishment of his capital, but the small-scale owner usually does not have the economic strength to invest for a distant future. The economic possibilities are summarized in Figure 17.

Much of this poorer forest land is held by private owners for "nonpecuniary" reasons. On many farms there is a patch of woodland which just is part of the farm without producing anything of consequence; the geometric layout in quarter-sections, etc., made many farms include odd corners of rough land unsuitable for cultivation. Such odd bits of forest are often too small even to sell, because they could not be consolidated into large forest parcels. Many other small forest parcels are owned for recreational purposes, or out of sentiment because the land has long been in the family, or in hope of speculative gain of land value, or as a hedge against inflation, or for some other reasons not connected with the productivity of the forests. In some cases, especially in the East, a small forest holding is an old family farm which no longer pays to farm but reverts to tree growth. Most of these small forest holdings are not remunerative possessions at present; their future potential is, of course, very different from one case to the other.

A NATIONAL POLICY FOR SMALL PRIVATE FORESTS

The question has been much discussed whether the nation needs the increased output of forest products which might result if the small privately owned forests were placed under better management to enhance their productivity. The United States Forest Service has studied the matter and concluded that the output of these small forests must be stepped up. Some private analysts have agreed, but the forest industry, by and large, does not believe that an increased output from the small forests will be seriously needed within the foreseeable future.

110

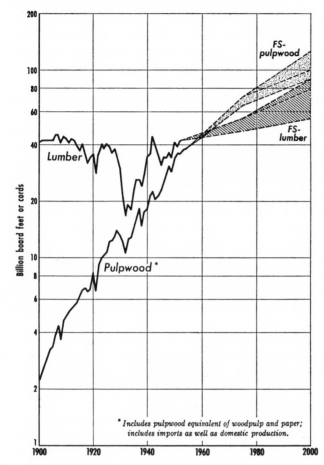

FIG. 18—LUMBER AND PULPWOOD CONSUMPTION, 1900–1955,
AND ALTERNATIVE PROJECTIONS, 1975 AND 2000

Lumber is one major raw material whose consumption has not risen
as national population and income have increased over the past fifty
years; it has gradually been replaced by other construction materials.
Paper, on the other hand, is an increasingly necessary part of our
complex modern economy and society.

If it were accepted that the level of output from small forest holdings should be stepped up, how could this be done? In the past, the answer most often heard was that the small forest owners should be educated to higher efficiency in forest management. The assumption was that the level of productivity in these forests was low because the owners did not practice good forestry, and that this was because they did not know how to do so. Educational efforts in the past have reached only a very small fraction of the private forest owners and seem not to have been very effective. If economic gains from good forestry have been less than the costs, then forest owners have been wise, from their own standpoint, not to engage in the kind of forestry recommended to them by the experts. The difficulty has thus been more deep-seated than a mere lack of knowledge.

Another public program in the past, available to small and large private forest owners alike, has been co-operative forest fire prevention and control. Federal funds have been available to the states, some of the latter have supplemented these funds, and private owners have made varying amounts of co-operative effort. A whole community gains from effective fire control; burned-over forest areas injure a whole community, by their unsightliness if by nothing else. As a result of intensive fire prevention and control programs extending over many years, the damage to forests from fire today is less than the damage from insects and disease.

Some other programs have been available to small private forest owners. In a few cases technical help in actual forestry operations has been available. Seedlings for replanting have been distributed, either free or at a nominal cost. In some cases, forest industry firms, and not public agencies only, have provided such services. However, in total they have only reached a small fraction of the very large number of small private forest owners.

If the full physical potential of these forests is to be achieved, public programs on a vastly bigger scale than in the past appear necessary. What kind of programs to prefer has been much discussed. Various kinds of subsidies, grants, aids, and incentives might be offered; but whether they would fulfill the purpose appears uncertain. To do so they would have to reach at least a million small-scale forest owners, which would be difficult at best. A substantial incentive would have to be supplied, and this might be a very costly program. A differentiation would have to be made according to size of forest holding and inherent productivity of the land. Also, among the small holdings, the prospects are better the larger the holding.

CHAPTER 11

Urban Land Use and Control

How much land is in "urban" use is difficult to determine, among other things because there are several definitions of urban land. One definition refers to the city as a legal entity. The total surface of cities and incorporated towns is the urban area in the legal sense. It changes incessantly with the growth of cities and concomitant incorporation of new areas and also with decline and disappearance of some older small towns. For discussion of the economics of urban land use, we are sometimes more interested in the city as the area of specific land uses, some of which lie outside the legal limits of the city. At the same time, the legal city area often includes areas which are not, or at least not yet, placed in urban-type use. Such areas, of course, also occur between areas of urban use outside the legal area of the city. If these nonurban areas, intermingled with urban-use areas, have ceased to be used for agriculture or forestry (by reason of tax conditions, for instance, as often happens in the United States), then there is a real problem of definition. Areas held by speculators with the hope that they will in time "ripen" into development for urban use are in some sense already part of the urban land-use area, even though they as yet carry no visible signs of urban activities.

Depending on such variations in definition, estimates of urban land in the United States range from 15 to 40 million acres, or even more. This is not more than 1 to 2 percent of the total land area of the 48 contiguous states. The demand for urban land is growing rapidly, however, and the encroachment upon farm and forest land may become more than negligible within

114

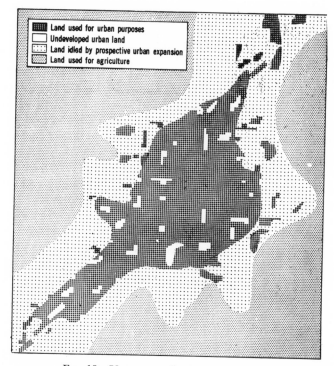

Legend:
- Land used for urban purposes
- Undeveloped urban land
- Land idled by prospective urban expansion
- Land used for agriculture

FIG. 19—URBAN AND SUBURBAN LAND USE

The typical city contains a good deal of idle land; even greater is the area of land idled around its periphery, waiting for later urban expansion. Much land is taken out of agriculture or forestry long before it is needed for urban uses.

the life span of the next generation. Looking at the economic value of the urban areas, an entirely different proportion comes out. Nowadays, most of the capital in the United States is urban capital; farm land and buildings account for only a few percent of all productive assets in the country. Even though most of the urban capital consists of buildings and other fixtures, and inven-

115

tories, the market value of urban land (as distinct from land and buildings) may be of a similar magnitude as the value of all the farm and forest land in the country.

This, of course, has nothing to do with the initial or native fertility of the land and very little with the climatic characteristics of the place. The nearly exclusive source of land value in urban uses is site—the geometric relation between a given property and surrounding properties and the economic activity that goes on in the environment. In a more vague sense, something similar goes also for farm land, for the character of farming also depends a good deal on the economic environment in which it is carried on. But urban land use is much more strictly influenced by the character of the immediate neighborhood. City center activity, factories, apartment houses, family residences, etc., all influence and are in turn influenced upon by surrounding activities, and all in many cases require a somewhat homogeneous neighborhood to thrive, in a way that farms do not. Logically, then, public authorities in the cities have more to say over the use of private land, and what they do (or abstain from doing) can have a profound influence on the development of the city.

EFFECTS OF PUBLIC ACTION ON URBAN LAND USE

About one third of the urban area (however defined) in the United States is public property. Most of this land consists of streets and alleys, but some is used for parks, playgrounds, and other public areas. The proportion of public land is higher in small cities and towns than in large ones; the proportionate area of streets, in particular, goes down as city size increases. In most cities there is more publicly owned land than there is land used for residential purposes.

The location of publicly owned areas (parks, especially), their improvements, and their connection with other publicly

owned areas (streets, particularly) exercise a powerful effect upon the use of privately owned land. The character of the streets
has often been a factor leading to (or inhibiting) the growth of
suburbs, for instance. In numerous indirect ways, the use and
improvement of publicly owned land affects the kind of use that
is possible on intermingled privately owned land.

The general public, through its elected city governments, can
add to the fund of publicly owned or controlled land by means
of condemning privately owned land, when such land is needed
for a public purpose. This refers not only to land which the city
government intends to keep as public property, but also to land
that is needed, for instance, for public utilities or other activity
deemed essential to public welfare. The public powers also
exercise a more indirect influence over the use of privately
owned tracts by the services they provide. Sewers, water supply,
schools and other group or social services are particularly important to small tracts of privately owned land. The provision
of such services often has encouraged people to move into new
areas, for instance. In some cases, people have built houses on
privately owned land and thereafter demanded that public
services be extended to those areas.

City government exercises still more control over private
land use through zoning, subdivision control, and other regula-
tory measures. In many cases landowners are told which uses
are permitted and which are prohibited on their land. Minimum size of lots, distance by which buildings must be set back
from the street, and other similar regulations have a major
effect on land use and on the appearance of the neighborhood.
In some ways this narrows down the range of things which an
owner can do with his property; but in normal cases, the benefit
of protection to intended bona fide uses far outweighs the in-
convenience of restriction to some. The democratic process of
electing city governments provides the safety valve, should a
city government use its power to favor special interests rather
than those of the general public.

HOW URBAN LAND IS USED

The area of land per 100 residents runs as high as 30 acres for the average small town of less than 5,000 inhabitants. It gradually declines as the size of the city increases and is only 5 acres in the large cities of a quarter million or more inhabitants. Thus the intensity of land use increases with city size. The intensity of use rises for almost every type of land use. We have al-

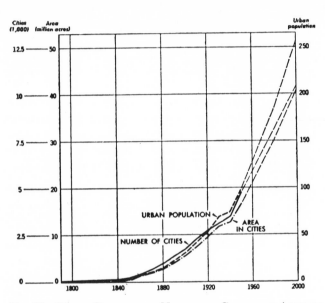

Fig. 20—Urban Population, Number of Cities, and Area of Cities in the United States, 1790–1950, and Projections to 2000

The number of cities, their area, and their population have increased at remarkably similar rates in the past, and promise to do so in the future. By the year 2000, each of these three measures will be at more than double its 1950 level. In the second half of the twentieth century, the problems of urban expansion may well be greater than they have been in all the past history of our country.

ready mentioned that the areas in streets and other public uses declines, relative to other land uses, as the size of the city increases. The intensity of land use also rises in the average residential area of cities of various size. In small cities, with less than 10,000 inhabitants, there are on the average about 12 to 14 people per acre of residential use; in cities of a quarter million or more total population, this proportion rises to 50 or more people, on the average. More people live in apartments, and the apartment houses average larger size, in the larger cities; more people also live in row houses, and even more in detached houses sitting on relatively small lots. There is also relatively less private garden area in the larger cities.

There are similar relationships for industrial and commercial land uses, even though the areas are not as large. As cities grow larger, the area of these intensive land uses increases, as does the intensity of their use. The development of suburbs has to some extent slowed down this process—as a consequence of more efficient transportation—but the main direction of these changes remains the same. Even the suburbs surrounding large cities sometimes use land more intensively than do the very small independent cities.

RACE, ECONOMIC CLASS, AND URBAN LAND USE

The older residential parts of most cities deteriorate physically, as the buildings get old and outdated. What were once fine houses and apartments become less attractive, and many people who can afford it move to newer housing areas. Sometimes only the younger generation moves out, but in time this has the same effect. As the higher income groups move out, they are replaced by lower income groups. The new inhabitants often crowd up more densely than the previous residents, and the aging properties are less well kept up. This downhill movement may continue until the area has become a slum. The

119

normal way out is by redevelopment, "slum clearance," and rebuilding with new buildings—usually of a different type than the old ones. Occasionally, a run-down neighborhood may be upgraded by means of refurbishing old buildings to luxury standards, on account of their aesthetic value, as has happened in Georgetown (Washington, D.C.); this is not uncommon in Europe, but in America it is as yet exceptional.

By the processes just mentioned, residential areas tend to get sorted and classified according to the economic class (income level) of their occupants. The separation by income is not absolute, but over the short run, it perpetuates itself, because the very class character of a neighborhood influences the price of its properties, thus helping to determine who can afford to live there. Low-income groups often pay a higher percentage of their income for housing than the high-income groups, and often get less in terms of space and amenities for each dollar spent; here as elsewhere in the world, poverty is an expensive proposition.

This sorting out of urban residential areas is complicated, in the United States, by racial discrimination. Many residents of higher income areas strive desperately to keep Negroes out, despite the fact that only the best educated and economically best placed Negroes could afford to buy property in such areas. Their measures have often been illegal and have proved effective in most cases. To a very great extent, the Negroes have been bottled up in the central cities; irrespective of his economic and social achievement, the Negro is usually forced to live in a neighborhood of more or less outspoken slum character, or at best in a ghetto of decent but low-income apartment houses. As southern Negroes migrate to cities in all parts of the country, a Negro neighborhood often starts with a "block-busting": some enterprising real-estate operator buys housing for Negro clients in a "white" neighborhood. The surrounding "white" residents foresee a fall in property values, some of them panic and sell hurriedly to move elsewhere, remaining "whites" see their apprehensions confirmed and also move away, often selling their properties at very low prices. The "block-busting" real-estate operator realizes a fat profit as he buys all these houses and resells them to Negro customers at considerably higher prices, all of which is possible because the customary discrimination creates an artificial shortage of housing for Negroes. The whole phenomenon of "block-busting" is possible because there is discrimination. In a few cases, where "white" residents did not run away in panic, the arrival of a few well-to-do Negro residents had no deteriorating effect either on the character of the neighborhood or on property values; the latter might even rise, because the removal of discrimination means the removal of a market restriction.

SLUMS AND URBAN RENEWAL

The end product of deteriorating urban areas is a slum. The process feeds on itself, for the existing slum areas are not just assembly space for those who are for other reasons the least fortunate in society. Those who grow up in a slum also become less well equipped to advance in a competitive society. If slums are just left to themselves, they will become the focal points for a downgrading of larger and larger segments of the urban population; to compound the problem, people living in slum conditions tend to have large families more often than happens in better housing areas.

In the past thirty years or so, slum removal and urban renewal programs have been applied, to a varying extent, in the United States. Such programs have removed some of the worst slum areas in many large cities. In spite of considerable public subsidy, the land values after clearing have been so high that the only kind of housing which seems economical is high-rise apartment buildings, that is, with high intensity of land use. And despite all efforts, including some subsidization, such apartments are usually suitable for middle-income families, not for those of the lowest income. The slum dwellers are thus pushed out to other areas, which then in turn deteriorate into slums. The charge has been made that slum clearance programs create as many new slums as they remove old ones.

More recently public programs have been undertaken to help people in the "gray" areas, those lying between the slums and the suburbs, maintain the physical condition and sociological character of their areas. This often involves measures for physical repair, modernization, and improvement of the properties; but it also involves a different attitude toward housing and living than has often prevailed in the past. Many of the people who live in such areas lack the financial resources to carry out these programs; more importantly, the will to do so and the leadership to organize people are also lacking. Because of the interrelationship between one family and the environment, an individual family is sharply limited in what it can do alone. Maintenance of a neighborhood is a group undertaking; unless there are group organizations and a group spirit, it probably cannot succeed. It is too soon yet to tell how well these new programs may work out.

INCOME AND TAXATION

Slums exist primarily because many people are poor; but as pointed out above, slums also breed poverty because of the deprived cultural environment in which the slum-dwellers' children are reared. Part of the answer to massive slum formation then is in raising incomes for the poorest strata of society, at least for those large segments of the poor who can be effectively rehabilitated.

Yet another facet of slum formation comes from the tax systems. When cities "rot from within," there must be some specific cause. The normal rules of economic location would tend to upgrade areas close to city center, but in recent times this has happened more often through subsidized slum clearance projects than through the spontaneous working of economic forces in the market place.

Some of the blame may be on the system of real-estate taxation, which places a tax on a piece of real estate in direct proportion to its market value (the "ad valorem" real estate tax). This often works out as a penalty on maintenance and improvements and also on the building of beautiful buildings, which may require more outlay for design and materials. The effect is usually not seen so much in the better residential areas, but is obvious both in city centers and in apartment-building areas in many American cities. A landlord, renting out "income property," will make no more improvements than he has to in order to collect the rent, and this means upkeep on the low side. Much "urban wasteland" is unused because farmers cannot afford the tax rates imposed by the city and therefore sell their land to speculators earlier than they otherwise would.

The effect is especially evident in slum areas. "Slumlords" often avoid making any repairs at all, unless they are forced to by legal means. This creates an artificial shortage of housing for decent, relatively low-income people who may then have to put up with slum conditions even though their own economic and personal standard is in fact somewhat better. A remedy might be in modifying the real-estate tax, either lowering it generally, or making it a flat rate on the land only irrespective of how it is built up (the line advocated by Henry George and his followers), or, less radically, by placing a lower tax rate on improvements, thus making it less forbidding to keep up income property or to build new structures to a high standard of comfort and aesthetics. A system of this kind is at work in cities in Pennsylvania and is credited with part of the success in recent urban-renewal programs (notably downtown Pittsburgh).

Another tax problem connected with slum formation is that of capital gains versus income tax. "Slumlords" are usually persons of great wealth, for whom the income tax rate would be high. A technique not infrequently applied has been that of charging high depreciation on the run-down old apartment houses to offset rental income and thus evading the income tax; after some years, the property is sold, maybe to another slumlord, and the purchase price (or its excess over the undepreciated value, if any) is returned as capital gains and taxed at a rate not exceeding 25 percent. These practices made the ownership of income property in urban slums exceedingly lucrative. Recent legislation provides for recapture of some "fast depreciation" and its taxation as ordinary income.

This American experience points to the profound effect that a tax system may have on the economic and social structure in a community and on its improvement or deterioration. Many argue that taxes are for revenue, not for ordering people about. The trouble is that any tax system, even one designed solely to produce revenue, will have economic effects, thus will "order people about" if by default rather than design. The real estate tax system "ad valorem" was invented when the country had a much simpler economic system. The beginning of a revision in Pennsylvania is symptomatic of the need for different tax systems in a complex urban economy.

CHAPTER 12

The Federal Domain in Recent Times

The whole early history of the federal domain was one of land disposal. Seldom if ever did the federal government contemplate using much of this land for its own direct purposes, nor were any early steps taken to determine what land the government would have to keep (because no one private person wanted it) or less still what land might be needed for public purposes in a distant future.

A reversal came only late in the nineteenth century, when the abundance of free land on the open frontier began to dry up. The Census of Agriculture showed, in 1880 for the first time, that a sizable part of all farmers (about one-fourth, at that time) were tenants, which pointed to the limitations of past land disposal programs as implementers of social ideals. At about the same time, prolonged experience of soil exhaustion in the older settled areas, as well of the climatic difficulties of the arid West, called to life the conservation movement. Changes in federal land policy, inspired by these and other contemporary trends of thought, were often brought about in a backhanded way; small groups of forward-thinking intellectuals pushed for certain reforms, but some of them were enacted because most politicians did not understand what they were about, rather than for the opposite reason. National parks, national forests, wildlife refuges, and grazing districts were established successively, to place the remaining federal domain under somewhat rational management. Purchase and exchange were sometimes used to expand the domain and modify its composition, to make it better meet its new purposes.

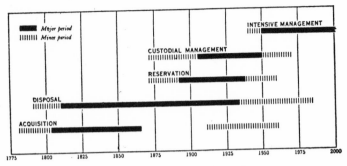

FIG. 21—MAJOR ERAS IN FEDERAL LAND OWNERSHIP AND
LAND MANAGEMENT IN THE UNITED STATES, 1800–2000

The processes of acquisition, disposal, reservation, and management
of federal lands have been partly separate and partly overlapping in
time.

NATIONAL PARKS, NATIONAL FORESTS, AND FEDERAL WILDLIFE REFUGES

The national park system started relatively early, with the
reservation of the Yellowstone National Park in 1872. The
special act of Congress by which that area was reserved long remained an imperfect law, for lack of means to enforce several of
its provisions. Land in the area could not be disposed of to individuals, and for such purpose it was as yet not very attractive;
but private hunting and game poaching went on as before for a
long time after the act. People knew little enough what they
wanted with a national park to discuss proposals to log its timber, or dam its major river to create an irrigation storage dam,
or otherwise use it for one practical purpose or another. Only
gradually were laws enacted, and even more slowly enforced,
which made the park what it is now intended for—a recreation
area; its popularity as such dates mainly from the time of World
War I.

Three more national parks were created in 1890: Yosemite,

126

General Grant and, Sequoia, all in California; to these were added Mount Rainier in 1899 and Crater Lake in 1902. Further parks were created in the Dakotas and in Oklahoma in 1903 and 1906, now promoted more by local vested interests than by a real idea of national parks. A long list of national parks has been added thereafter, beginning with Mesa Verde in 1906 and continuing up to Virgin Islands and Petrified Forests parks in 1956 and 1958. The system was put in somewhat better order by an act (1916) establishing a National Park Service.

Other land areas have been reserved from economic use as national monuments, under an act passed in 1906. There are nearly a hundred of these today. They fall into five general groups: remains of prehistoric civilizations, historic relics, geologic examples, botanic reservations, and wild animal reservations. Most of these are small in area, but there are a few large ones. In a few cases, a national monument has been converted to a national park. There are also national seashores, national military parks, national historic sites, national cemeteries, and others. Most of the national parks and monuments were established out of the federal domain. Some have been created by private donations, especially in the East.

National forests cover much larger areas, generally, than national parks, and they have a more varied use, including several economic uses. The right of the President to reserve forest lands, so that they could not be detached from the federal domain, was established in 1891 after several unsuccessful attempts. The provisions of that and several subsequent bills were the focus of much bitter political controversy, and on several occasions the outcome of the struggle might have been different but for the combination of incidental happenings and the purposeful action of a few far-sighted individuals with drive and determination. Among these we can mention Gifford Pinchot, a young forester who masterminded the large-scale reservations of federal forests under President Theodore Roosevelt (1901–1909) and who succeeded in having the administration of these forests separa-

127

ted from the General Land Office. Desirable as was much of what Pinchot achieved, it also stirred up bitter controversy, split the ranks of the conservationists, and created rigid positions and vested interests which sometimes are embarrassing to this day.

Another aspect of the conservation movement was the preservation of wild game. Many species had been incredibly abundant as long as only the low-efficient weapons of the Indians kept them in check. Firearms permitted much more extensive killing; buffaloes were shot for their skins, the meat being left to rot, until the vast herds were reduced to small remnants. Some species, such as the passenger pigeon, were completely exterminated. To halt this destruction, conservationists began a drive to reserve some areas as wildlife refuges. Yellowstone Park was closed to hunting in 1894, and several states established wildlife refuges before or after that date. The first federal wildlife refuge was established in 1903, but for many years thereafter, only a few others were added. The big expansion of wildlife refuges came under President Franklin D. Roosevelt, partly by setting aside tracts of the federal domain, partly by buying land for the same purpose. Today there is a relatively extensive system of such areas, even though more may be needed if certain scarce species are to be preserved.

GRAZING DISTRICTS

In spite of the extensive withdrawals of land for permanent public use described above and in spite of continued disposal of land to individuals, there were, as late as in 1934, still more than 180 million acres of so-called open public domain (not counting Alaska). In principle this area was open to entry under the land laws. Land disposal had always been a selective process, and so was the setting aside of reservations for public use. Most of the federal domain that remained open in 1934 was suited only for grazing, and much of it was of low productivity even in such

128

use. Large parts of these areas were grazed by nearby ranchers, without any legal authorization of any kind.

Proposals for the orderly use of these lands were made as far back as in the 1880's. Some of them were unrealistic because they overestimated the productivity of these lands. Not until 1934, by the Taylor Grazing Act, were these lands placed under a permanent system of management. One important feature was the authority to classify these lands and to deny disposal except when classified as suitable for the purpose sought. Odd parcels could be sold, and other smaller areas could be leased for grazing. The major feature of the act was the provision for grazing districts, with licensing of livestock grazing and with a positive program of land management. In practice the grazing districts have been managed in ways similar to those applied to the national forests, although the use is here even less intensive.

PURCHASE AND EXCHANGE

Since the time when lands began to be permanently reserved for federal ownership, the government has also acquired land by purchase and by exchange. The first major purchase program was enacted in 1911 (the Weeks Act). The first national forests were all in the West, because that is where the remaining public domain lay. Interest in national forests in the East led to the passage of this act, under which more than 20 million acres have been purchased. In one unusual move the government recaptured a railroad grant in Oregon which had never been used for its purpose—an area of 2.5 million acres including some unusually valuable timber stands. Private enclaves within national parks were often acquired by purchase.

In the 1930's a different kind of federal land purchase program was established. Its purpose was to buy farm lands that were submarginal for continued farm operation and to convert them to grassland or forest. Some national forest lands were acquired in this manner, and the federal wildlife refuge areas were expanded in the same way; substantial areas were turned over to the states to be used as parks. Later, during World War II and after, the defense and atomic energy agencies have purchased extensive areas for their needs.

The federal government has sometimes acquired land through exchange (barter). Before World War II, the Forest Service also exchanged timber for land, but this type of exchange is no longer used. The total area involved in all types of exchange is relatively small, but locally some such transactions have been important.

THE SIZE OF THE PUBLIC DOMAIN

Information about public lands—those owned by the federal, state, county, city and other units of government—usually relates to acreage; very little is known about the value of these lands.

One third of the entire area of the United States is owned by the federal government. Some of it has always been so owned; other large areas have been acquired by purchase or exchange, and sometimes by donation, from private owners. Almost half of all the federal land is in Alaska, where nearly 99 percent of all the land still is the property of the federal government. In a very large part this reflects the fact that most of the land in the state is unused and has small prospects for intensive use in the foreseeable future.

Of the large federal estate, less than 4 percent is owned by defense agencies; the rest is held by various civil agencies. Of these, the Department of the Interior controls almost exactly two thirds of the total federal domain, the Department of Agriculture about one fourth. Two thirds of the land is predominantly for forestry and wildlife; slightly more than one fifth is mainly for grazing, with miscellaneous uses occupying the remainder.

The various states also own land. Part of this domain—

130

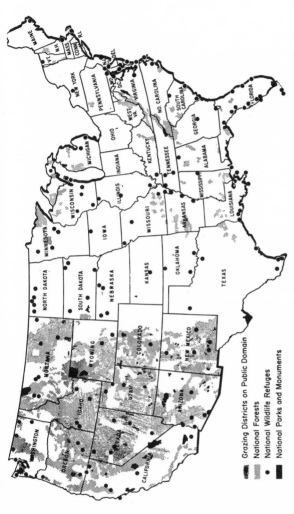

FIG. 22—FEDERAL LAND AREA OF THE FORTY-EIGHT CONTIGUOUS STATES

Over a third of all federal lands lie in Alaska, not shown on this map. A full half of the total lies in the Rocky Mountains and to their westward. This concentration of federal land ownership in certain regions is partly the result of land history, partly because the lands in question are not suited for agricultural uses.

about two thirds of the total—is the remainder of their original grants from the federal government; a lesser part results from land purchases for special purposes. States other than Alaska have received grants of 230 million acres of land; Alaska was given a grant which ultimately could include over 100 million acres, but only a fraction of this has as yet been transferred to the state. Altogether, the states now own somewhat more than 80 million acres. State land ownership is most common in the western United States, in the same regions where the federal domain has its largest expanses.

Cities and counties, and local units of government such as drainage districts, are also owners of considerable land areas. We lack precise and inclusive data about this type of public land ownership. Within cities, it appears that publicly owned land is the same proportion as in the nation as a whole—about one third of the total, and these areas are among the most intensively used in the country.

USES OF THE FEDERAL DOMAIN

As a result of the historical land disposal processes, the federal domain consists mainly of mountains, deserts, tundra, and other types of land whose productivity for agriculture is low or nil. The vast mountain chain of the Rockies and the Cascade-Sierra Nevada, as well as lesser mountain groups, are largely in the federal domain. The deserts of the Great Basin and of western Arizona–southeastern California are also almost entirely owned by the federal government. Most of the vast expanses of Alaska are either tundra or sparse forest.

Outdoor recreation is the use of federal lands which affects the largest number of people nowadays. In 1960, total visits to the national park system were 79 million, to the national forests 93 million, to federal wildlife refuges 11 million. Obviously the same persons often made more than one visit. It is equally obvious that those who take advantage of the recreational possibili-

132

ties of the federal domain amount to a large part of those who are in a position to do so (many are too young or too old, etc.). Probably about half of the total population have made some use of these areas in recent years.

People go to the federal land areas for many different kinds of outdoor recreation. Some are interested primarily in sight-seeing, perhaps without even leaving their cars. Others walk in the forest, picnic, swim, or camp overnight. Some engage in fishing, fewer in hunting; and a few strenuous individuals climb mountains, explore caves, or otherwise enjoy being in a rugged landscape.

The trend of these outdoor activities is steeply and regularly upward. In recent years, total use has generally been 10 percent larger than the preceding year. The basic reasons are increasing population, higher real incomes per person, more leisure, and better transportation.

Grazing by livestock is another important use of the federal lands. In the regions where there are extensive federal land areas, a substantial proportion of all ranchers graze their livestock on such lands at some season. Even though the total amount of forage obtained in this way is not very large, it is often strategic because the grazing takes place at a particular season when it is badly needed. Grazing districts provide forage at different seasons, but not always to the same stock owners. For instance, a rancher may obtain winter grazing on the desert for his sheep or spring and fall grazing for either cattle or sheep, or in some cases summer grazing for either class of livestock, but rarely for all three, or even two, seasons. Intricate patterns of private and public land use have arisen because of these seasonal factors. Grazing use of national forests has been declining for many years; on the grazing districts, it has been rather stable.

Another important use of some federal lands is timber harvest, especially on the national forest. The demand for the timber from the federal forests is higher now than it was at the time when privately owned timber land was more abundant and easier of access. So much of the private timber land now belongs to large timber processors, that access to supplies from the federal forests has become especially important to the smaller processors, as well as others who do not own any forest land. The large part of all mature timber (40 percent, recently) that is found on the federal domain underlines their importance for competitive marketing. The total volume of timber sold from federal lands has climbed rapidly in recent years. Before World War II, about 2 billion board feet were cut annually from the federal forests; today, the annual cut is roughly 9 billion board feet. Other publicly owned forest lands have seen their annual cut increase somewhat more slowly. The sustained yield of the public forests, under optimum management, could be as high as 15 to 20 billion board feet annually. The prices of timber from the federal forests have also risen sharply in recent time.

Federal lands are also leased for private exploration for economically exploitable minerals, especially oil and gas. Most of such leases are what is called "wildcat" operations; the lessee hopes that he, or someone else, will drill for oil and gas, but much leased land is never drilled, and much that is drilled yields no oil. However, substantial revenue is obtained from such leases, primarily from royalties from the producing ones (usually one eighth of the value of output.) Federal lands are also leased for coal, potash, sodium, and other mineral development. In addition, private persons may obtain title to land for other mineral development, such as gold, silver, lead, copper, uranium, and other metals.

Federally owned lands are also important elements in watershed development schemes. A substantial proportion of all stream flow in the West originates on national forests. The grazing lands at lower elevations often contribute heavily to the sediment load in streams. Many municipalities get their water supply from federally owned watersheds. Protection of these and other watersheds from fire and erosion is a highly important purpose of federal land management.

GOVERNMENT PROCESSES FOR FEDERAL LAND MANAGEMENT

The general public obtains use of federal lands and their products under a wide variety of arrangements. Anyone is free to use any public recreation area—sometimes with payment of a small fee, often without charge. Within most federal properties one may also use other areas than those designated for recreation, if one observes a few simple rules and precautions about fire and other hazards. Most timber is sold at competitive sale, and so are mineral leases on proven productive areas. Most mineral leases are noncompetitive, however: the first applicant is awarded the lease. Grazing permits and leases are not sold competitively; applicants must own property on which the livestock is kept during the rest of the year when not on federal land. In practice, grazing leases and permits tend to remain with owners of the same properties for long periods.

The federal land management agencies each have a central office in Washington. Each also has regional or state offices, or both, and each has local offices, on or near the land being managed. Because the federal lands are spread over such a wide area, the local offices have broad discretionary authority to act within a framework of general rules and regulations laid down in Washington.

Funds for management of the federal lands are obtained through the rather intricate and lengthy budgeting-appropriation-expenditure process generally used in the federal administration. The budget is specified in considerable detail, with many separate amounts earmarked for specific purposes. The main difference in contrast to private business administration is in the way investment decisions are handled and investment expenditures accounted for. Funds for investment are treated the same as current expenditures and written off immediately. This precludes any judgment as to the profitability (or lack of it) of a given investment, and also renders it more difficult to obtain funds for purposes which may be profitable over a long period in the future. A separate capital account would help to clarify what is really going on, economically speaking, in the management of public property.

Products and uses of federal lands are priced to users under a wide variety of arrangements. Timber and some mineral leases are sold competitively, as noted above. With these exceptions, all uses of federal lands are on terms more favorable than would be available from private landowners. Grazing fees are much lower than rentals of private grazing land, even when allowance is made for the substantial differences in productivity. Noncompetitive mineral leases are usually at a lower rate than is paid for private lands in the same localities. Recreation areas are free or nearly so. Some of the complexities of federal land management might be simplified if the principles of competitive business were more consistently applied. Federal agencies are restrained from doing this because of law, custom, or their own caution. Low prices and free use undoubtedly encourage more use than would otherwise take place, and sometimes there is also more careless and destructive use in this way.

The federal lands are managed by a large and expanding corps of professional people, usually with college or university training. As a branch of the civil service, these people have on the whole high standards both of professional competence and personal integrity. Many are highly specialized in one function or another. Those who handle economic decisions (price of timber, volume of timber or grazing available, for instance) face private counterparts who are prepared to drive hard bargains. The human type represented by the civil servant in charge of economically valuable goods and services is widely different from the rugged frontier individualists who were the principal users of the federal domain a hundred years ago and

136

even later. The scope of this service is a consequence of the decisions taken around the turn of the century about reservation of federal land as permanent government property.

Apart from the very size of the public domain, the level of demand for its products and services is, of course, another determinant of the scope of activity that has to be handled by the managing agencies and their staff. The increasing demand for timber on the national forests was mentioned above. The relation between demand and management activity is especially evident in regard to the use of public land for outdoor recreation. As long as there were few tourists or campers, land managers had little bother on their account. With the high and rapidly mounting demand for outdoor recreation in many areas today, the public land manager must cope with this high demand. He cannot refuse to accept recreationists unless he is prepared to take the drastic step of closing roads to visitors. The numbers of visitors, and the activities they seek, will go far to determine the manpower and expenditures necessary to manage the area properly, and this is usually the basis on which he asks for increased appropriation of funds. The changes of the public's tastes and wishes and the size of income they can dispose of will set the limits, step by step, for the job of managing the public lands.

CHAPTER 13

Outlook—In Time and Space

This book has sought to give a brief and highly generalized history of the land system of the United States, as it was evolved by white men, in part assisted by black and yellow manpower, and in conflict with the red men of the continent's aboriginal population. Rather than a chronological account of events, we have tried to give a systematic survey of issues and solutions in the building up of this land system, and with more emphasis on the institutional than on the technical aspects of land holding and land use. There is a vast literature available on the details of all the various partial problems. In this chapter we will try to evaluate, in the broadest terms, the usefulness of this system to the country—past, present, and future—and to indicate what lessons, if any, that other countries may draw from the experience of the United States in this area.

The story of the United States land system in its historical setting is in a large measure a success story. The detailed account shows many oddities, complexities, and failures, and much waste; but the pervasive features have been expansion and growth under a modicum of order in essential respects and with a basic framework of democratic institutions.

We have emphasized the importance of the colonial period and its antecedents in the Old World of Western Europe. Colonial society, small as it was, created many of the determinants for modern development in North America. From that period came both the frontier spirit and the idea of orderly disposal of vacant land—land to become the property of the many, not just the few. This massiveness of the land disposal movement must in itself have contributed to the relatively very systematic and accurate (by the standards of the epoch) methods of land description and survey which turned out to be so important for the relative orderliness of the land disposal process no less than for continued evolution of the land system across an essentially free land market. In one respect as the other, the less complete application of the same principles in some southeastern states only underscores how essential were these features of democracy and order in the land disposal process. The arrangement with all or most vacant land being federal domain later became the starting point for one of the innovations to the system in recent time, when areas not suited for individual ownership were permanently reserved as federal property.

The story of the past was principally one of creating a system for holding and using farm land. The outlook for the United States itself presents few critical problems. The survey systems permit smooth adaptation to the needs of larger farm units, and the creation of these will further facilitate the necessary works of soil conservation which sometimes ran into problems on account of the rectangular layout; soil conservation districts and other group or area arrangements have since long taken care of much the same set of problems. Present land tenure conditions, as they have evolved gradually from the original patterns of predominant ownership by operators, also are more functional in a capital-intensive economy than is sometimes understood by those whose enthusiasm for owner-farmers is grounded in the conditions of a capital-scarce, preindustrial or early-industrial economic system.

For the conditions of a market economy, the United States farm land system is essentially satisfactory. Anything in the world bears some improvement, but the farm land system of the country presents no fatal flaws.

How justified such a judgment is can sometimes be elucidated by comparison with other countries, and the countries under comparison can then also draw some conclusions in the inverse

139

direction. The contrast is less sharp than sometimes believed if comparison is made with Western Europe. The part of the Old World from which most of the colonial and early nineteenth-century immigrants came was not static; it was generating and it was participating in, if slower, the same processes that created a democratic society in North America at such an accelerated pace. Today the farm land systems of Western Europe are not so different from that of the United States; there is more regulation on account of tighter economic situations, but Western European farmers are in many ways placed much as their American counterparts were a few decades earlier and are advancing along a similar path of progress. The rectangular layout is exceptional, but land registration and other administrative arrangements are ready to serve the land markets that exist.

Comparison with preindustrial countries in Asia and Africa would be unfair for a great many reasons. Countries of recent settlement should lend themselves more directly to comparison. Those colonized by England (Canada, Australia, New Zealand) have systems with much the same general characteristics as that of the United States, if with many differences in detail. The contrast with Latin America is extremely instructive in a way that both sides should be able to learn from.

A FEW SHARP CONTRASTS WITH LATIN AMERICA

Apart from a few islands and small coastal areas in the Caribbean, all the countries south of the Rio Grande were colonized by Spain and Portugal. The two countries had essentially similar cultural and political situations, and even though some differences between them are important enough in themselves, we have no strong reason to dwell upon these differences here.

For one thing, the Iberian countries occupied their parts of the Western Hemisphere about a century before English colo-

140

nists began to take hold in North America. The time was less rife with new ideas and possibilities than the following century, and the two Iberian monarchies, just emerging from the late phase of liberation from the Moors, were rather conservative in outlook and aristocratic in structure. During the colonization period, the Catholic reaction of "counterreformation" further strengthened the backward looking, nonevolutive character of Iberian society. The impact on Latin America was twofold. Old densely settled areas of peasant farming in Mexico, Guatemala, and the Andean countries of South America were simply placed under new overlords. The presence of downtrodden peons, accustomed to hard work for poor living under close regimentation, inspired a takeover rather than any innovation. Although the colonizing monarchies did not have any genuine feudalism themselves, the imposition of local landlords with vast possessions in land and people, with scant possibility for supervision by a distant central authority, led to many "quasifeudal" conditions, among them virtual peonage. In the vast empty areas outside the old Indian civilizations, by contrast, the whole settlement movement was slow and gave quantity results only at an even later date than in North America. In the tropics of Brazil and Venezuela, the resulting system was one of plantations, with African slave labor—an extreme variant of the southern plantation system of the United States. In temperate areas, foremost in Argentina, the abundance of land was hastily grabbed up by a small number of landlords claiming vast areas each. Very extensive grazing systems then also laid the bases for an aristocratic structure of land ownership, with subsequent lack of opportunity for the many when immigration gathered momentum in the late part of the nineteenth century.

All of these failures are sometimes blamed on the kings of Spain and Portugal. Their failure was by default rather than intent, though; the land laws actually on the books were far better than their application, which is often overlooked when modern people look at their impact on the land systems in southwestern United States, for instance. The forcelessness of the crown left local landlords virtually unlimited power, and they used it for perpetuating their own wealth, not for the development of their countries. Wealth generated on South American plantations was too often placed—and squandered—in Europe. No land offices were needed to accommodate a land disposal process whereby the leading families, in possession of the central government of ostensibly republican nations, disposed of vacant land to themselves and their relatives. The immigrant landing in Brazil or Argentina found no opportunity other than working for wages which were low in countries where economic development was held back by the very same forces that exploited their labor. At the root of it all is the land system, which lacked fluidity and virtually prevented the creation of a population of independent, family-scale farmers. Exceptions to these rules exist—in southern Brazil, for instance, in the areas of German and Japanese settlement—and they complete the evidence as to the coercive power of the land system over the entire development of economy and society.

As a legacy of all this delayed and archaic-minded development, most Latin American countries have land systems which are very unsatisfactory and widely recognized as such. Land reform is the very issue of reform in most of these countries; its partial success in Mexico and its early difficulties in Bolivia are widely cited as pros and cons in a debate which really is about the whole future of Latin society. Apart from making the size of landholdings less unequal, land reform also will need to improve the land market and credit systems, in order to render land and capital effectively available for a land market after the reform. It also will have to spend a considerable educational effort to upgrade peasant populations whom the archaic land system held down on an extremely low economic and cultural level; only then will these people become capable of using the new economic opportunity which a land reform makes available in principle.

The alternatives to land reform are also controversial. Many believe that without land reform, these countries are inevitably heading for Communist revolutions. Others hope that the issue can be bypassed by accelerating industrial development and by hastening the transition to large-scale, highly mechanized agriculture. Those who follow the latter reasoning usually overlook the quantity aspects of both industrialization and agricultural mechanization, and especially of transforming illiterate, downtrodden, high birth-rate peasant masses into a modern industrial population. Most serious analyses, for most of these countries, point to land reform as an indispensable alternative to political catastrophe.

Ironically enough, some of the resistance against land reform —both in Latin America and in the United States—point to the United States land system as a counterargument. Such a reasoning overlooks the difference in historical situation. The United States had a land reform from the outset—in the very way the public domain was once settled. From that starting point, United States land institutions have continued to fulfill their role satisfactorily on the whole. Most parts of Latin America have not even reached the starting point from which the whole modern development of the United States took place. Latin latifundia are frequently much larger than any plantations in the southern United States, and the idea of large-scale mechanization is premature in most of those countries.

A LOOK AHEAD

Even though the United States land system has on the whole served well in the past and continues to do so at present, no system remains sound without continuous outlook for the perspectives of change. It was mentioned above that the farm land system appears to remain serviceable for long periods into the future. Some modifications in the tenure systems may be anticipated, especially with a view to secure adequately sized holdings without burdening the farmer with exorbitant downpayments on a mortgage debt. Other problems with regard to farm land tenure, at least in the medium-term future, regard the apparent necessity to withdraw some of the least productive farm land from production. How to achieve this without inflicting crushing economic damage on individuals is one policy issue to decide about, gradually as the problem unfolds—and if it does unfold. The land purchase program on the Great Plains in the 1930's was a partial answer, although short-lived. Some program of a similar kind, and on a voluntary basis, is at work in New York State, as an aid in converting low-grade farm land into forest. With the large population increase that is anticipated for the United States during the rest of this century, the surplus problem may not require as much land retirement as is now believed.

Forest resources are another of those resource problems which are often believed to need policy action to meet the needs of the future. This overlooks the fact that the actual demand for forest products is much more a function of the cost of timber and of other materials which can serve the same needs; a shortage would be solved through changes in relative prices much more than through any physical lack of material. Even so it remains a policy issue how far the country should go in investing toward higher productivity of forest land, both for timber production and for meeting the demands for recreational space.

The most pressing land problems of the future are in fact likely to be those of space for living, communication, and leisure. Urban land, highways and other traffic space, and recreational areas are land uses that will expand more than proportionately to population growth, if *per caput* income continues to rise. The cities can no longer be left to rot from within, nor will subsidized rebuilding programs be sufficient if the forces that make for slum formation are left unabated. Both the real estate tax and the systems for capital gains tax as an alternative to income tax may have to be reformed, to allow for systems of urban land

144

use more in line with the needs of the burgeoning, more and more affluent population, and to prevent slum formation from inflicting lasting damage to those segments of the population that are or become caught in the vicious circle of poverty. Residential and other land uses by persons will need to be integrated, as a means of restoring to the land market the degree of freedom of which prejudice and segregation have robbed it. The complementary nature of transportation by car, truck, bus, subway, railroad, and airplane will have to be brought into more harmony to permit people and goods to get from here to there with minimum waste and minimum loss of freedom. The beauty of cities, roadsides, and the open landscape must be protected against ugly buildings, scrap and litter, billboards, and picnic refuse. All of this will require tax reform, legislation on permissible land use, and education of the public.

All this sounds like a formidable list of problems to solve. Anyone who cares can make the list much, much longer. But basically a free society has the tools to obtain the change it wishes. The inherited land system of the United States has its faults, but on the whole it is a good framework on which to introduce further improvements.